Contents

Introduction

In today's rapidly changing world we are more aware than ever of the need to teach children how to learn for themselves. Recent developments in science and technology make us believe that it is essential that children develop skills and attitudes which enable them to learn, rather than acquiring a large body of facts which rapidly become outdated and thus irrelevant.

By teaching children **how** to learn we are giving them the opportunity to develop problem-solving skills which will serve them throughout their lives. This growing awareness of the importance of encouraging children to develop their investigative skills is highlighted in recent documents, including those quoted below.

We have designed this material to meet identified needs and to encourage children to develop science skills from an early age. Extensive trialling has shown that children enjoy the open-ended nature of the problems and we have set the problems in interesting contexts which appeal to children. By making sure that the activities are relevant to the children and build upon previous experiences we feel that they will help children to answer questions which are important to them, such as:

- How does it . . . ?
- What will happen if . . . ?
- Why do you think that . . . ?

We believe that these activities will encourage children to be more inquisitive and develop their manipulative, cognitive and reasoning skills. The material which is designed to be used as a flexible resource rather than a course in itself will, we believe, widen children's problem-solving skills in a variety of ways. We also believe that the activities will help you to show your children that science and technology are important, relevant and **fun**!

David Rowlands
Carol Holland

Quotations from recent documents

'All class teachers, without exception, should include some science in their teaching . . . in a way which emphasises practical, investigative and problem-solving activity.'

'An introduction to scientific method . . . offers practical opportunities . . . for the solving of problems in an everyday context.'

'Pupils should develop the art of seeking possible solutions and evaluating them.'

DES Science 5–16: A Statement of Policy

'Pupils should develop design and technology capability by exploring familiar situations. They should also look at familiar things as starting points for some of their design and technological activities.

Within the general requirements of design and technology, activities should encourage the appraisal of artefacts, systems and environments made by others . . . (and) . . . pupils should have increasing opportunities for more open-ended research, leading to the identification of tasks for designing and making.

Technology in the National Curriculum: DES 1990

'[Schools] should encourage the active exploration of the environment and opportunities for children to interact with objects and materials.'

'Science education should provide opportunities for all pupils to develop an understanding of key concepts and enable them to be used in unfamiliar situations. To allow this to happen, pupils need to understand and explore their use in a range of contexts . . . . All pupils should be enabled to learn and use scientific methods of thinking.'

'There is an essential role for the teacher as enabler . . . the teacher may interact with the pupil, raise questions, build in appropriate challenges and experiences, and offer new ways of thinking.'

Science in the National Curriculum: DES 1989

1 The aims of these activities

Aims

- To develop children's problem-solving abilities.
- To develop children's skills and attitudes in co-operative group work.
- To develop children's skills in planning investigations.
- To develop children's skills in predicting and fair testing.
- To develop children's manipulative skills to allow them to design, make and modify devices and working models.
- To develop children's communication skills using different media.
- To stimulate curiosity and develop children's research skills in order to broaden their view of science and technology.
- To involve the use of simple, safe and familiar equipment and materials.
- To encourage an appreciation of the relevance of science and technology to everyday life.
- To encourage an awareness that the applications of science and technology have social implications.
- To appeal equally to boys and girls of all cultural backgrounds.
- To encourage an awareness that the learning process is more significant than the end result.

2 What is problem-solving?

The processes of problem-solving

Problem-solving is a part of our lives and it is an essential skill for every future citizen which can only be learned by first-hand experience. Although problems may be different and diverse, they are best tackled in an organised way using a range of process skills. These process skills can include:

1 discussing, researching and proposing solutions to a problem
2 planning and carrying out an investigation to solve a problem, **or** designing and building a device to meet the criteria set in a problem
3 testing, evaluating and modifying the device or solution to perform better.

For example, Challenge 22 *The long drop* has been chosen to illustrate one approach. The children are asked to make a parachute which will allow a 5 g Plasticine ball to fall 2 metres as slowly as possible. The process they might go through is as follows:

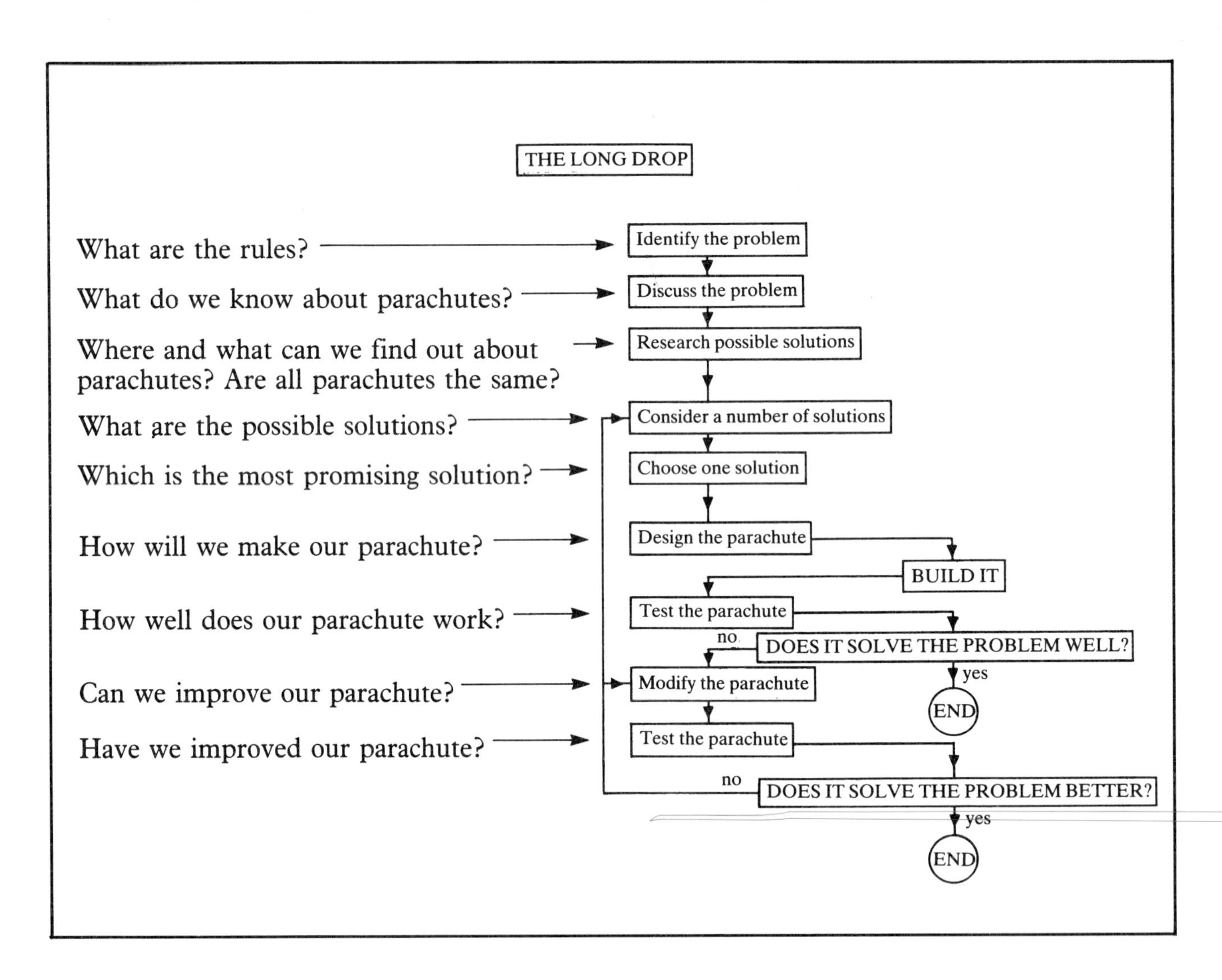

3 What does this pack contain?

This pack contains all that you need to use problem-solving activities with children in the primary classroom. It is organised into three main components:

1 There is an introduction and general description of the activities giving advice on the use of these challenges and indicating their potential to deliver aspects of the National Curriculum for Science and for Technology.

2 The 48 activities are presented as copyright-free master sheets. The sheets are designed as a flexible resource from which teachers can select appropriate activities and integrate them into a topic or theme of work. They are **not** intended to be used in isolation but rather as part of a broad and varied approach to teaching.

The activities cover nine widely-taught topic areas:
- Measuring things
- Water
- Structures and machines
- Air
- Separating things
- Electricity and magnetism
- Heat
- Colour and light
- Materials

Each topic area is covered by a selection of activities. All the worksheets have the following common features:
- a lively and interesting title
- text which presents the challenge clearly and precisely using carefully controlled language
- illustrations which are presented with humour and which provide hints and clues to the challenge.

3 On the opposite page of each master sheet are the detailed teaching notes to go with that activity. Each activity's teaching notes provide the following information:

A Specific aims
These aims, dealing with **skills** and **concepts**, are written to clarify the teaching aims of each challenge.

B Equipment per group
In an ideal teaching situation we might hope to see a group of children being presented with a challenge and, after thought and discussion, producing a list of equipment which would allow them to tackle the challenge. Given time, the equipment listed by each group could be gathered together ready for children to test their ideas at the first opportunity. This is an excellent approach in that it prevents children looking for 'answers' in the equipment provided. However, it does put considerable strain on a teacher's time and resources.

One strategy which can be used to ease the problem is to ask children to bring in material from home. In this way you can establish a junk box containing a wide variety of bits and pieces which 'might be useful one day'. Many of these bits and pieces most certainly will be useful when the children are involved in problem-solving activities. The range of materials can include yoghurt pots, scrap card, plastic bottles, cloth, wood, packaging, etc. These bits and pieces can be stored tidily and cheaply in large, plastic dustbins.

Another approach to the organisation of the equipment is to use the detailed list given in the teaching notes to prepare a set of materials which children might need to use with a particular challenge. Having this material ready-prepared helps considerably in getting a group started on an activity. However, it must be stressed that children should not feel constrained to just the materials provided.

Generally the challenges use cheap, readily available materials which are already used in primary schools. There are some exceptions which involve constructional activities using commercial products such as LEGO Technic 1 kits, Somertech kits or Meccano. These flexible and well designed products are a valuable classroom resource and provide many of the components needed to realise the children's designs. A list of suppliers is given in the *Resources* section.

In a number of activities digital stop-watches and weighing machines are specified and recommended because they are easy to use and read, and relatively sturdy.

C Notes

These notes are a compilation of the experiences of teachers in using the activities. The more common solutions to each challenge are described, although by no means are all the possibilities covered. The very nature of the challenges makes it impossible to predict all the possible solutions and in many cases it is the unusual and unexpected solutions which make using the material so rewarding.

Details of possible extension activities are given along with ideas on presenting the challenges to different age groups.

Safety problems are highlighted and these are dealt with in more detail in the *Safety* section in Chapter 5 (p. 16).

Finally an indication is given of the topics and themes where particular activities have been used successfully.

D Key vocabulary

A list of important words is given for each activity.

E National Science Curriculum analysis

In this analysis we have identified the potential areas of delivery of the National Science Curriculum. The analysis has been made in terms of Statements of Attainment within relevant Attainment Targets, with components of a Statement of Attainment being identified by a suffix a) or b) etc.

For example, within Attainment Target 3: Processes of life, the first component of level 2 'know that living things reproduce their own kind' is described as AT3, level 2a), while the third component 'to be able to give a simple account of the pattern of their own day' is described as AT3, level 2c).

Although our analysis, for reasons of clarity, has centred on the Statements of Attainment, we feel it is essential that teachers absorb the relevant section of the Programme of Study and interpret the latter at the level of the child (or children) working in the classroom.

F National Technology Curriculum analysis

As with the previous analysis, this table cross-references each activity to specific Statements of Attainment within the four Technology Attainment targets. Again it is essential to absorb the relevant sections of the Programme of Study in order to gain a full understanding of the style of delivery to children demanded by the National Technology Curriculum.

4 How do these activities assist the National Curriculum?

The National Science Curriculum

The main purpose of the implementation of the National Curriculum in Science and Technology is to ensure that **all** children experience science as a continuum. By selecting appropriate challenges within this pack it is possible for teachers to choose activities which build upon previous experiences and which help children to develop their knowledge, understanding and skills in science. Appropriate challenges will also provide an ideal forum for children to show understanding of skills and concepts and could therefore be used by teachers as assessment opportunities to provide evidence in building up a child's science profile during and at the end of key stages.

An essential requirement of the National Science Curriculum is that children enjoy a well-balanced, broad programme of study which is relevant to their needs and interests. We believe that these challenges provide links with the real world, making it possible to deliver, in a child-centred way, the framework established by the Programmes of Study for key stages 1 and 2. At the end of each key stage i.e. at ages 7 and 11 the children will be assessed and assigned a specific 'level' for science based on the two Profile Components:

Profile Component 1 – The Exploration of Science (AT 1)

The whole ethos of science is process based. If children are to make any progress in skill development continued re-inforcement of problem-solving skills is crucial. We believe that these activities give children the opportunities to hypothesise, putting forward their own suggestions and ideas; to design and plan investigations, building up their experiences in controlling variables; to carry out explorations by selecting and using appropriate measuring instruments and equipment; to record their investigations using a wide variety of techniques; to draw conclusions from these results and to communicate their findings. This will enable the children to meet the requirements laid out in the statements of Attainment in AT1.

Profile Component 2 – Knowledge and Understanding ATs (2–6, 9–16)

The context through which children demonstrate the scientific skills outlined in AT 1 are described in Profile Component 2. It is essential that children visit and revisit the relevant Programmes of Study to ensure competence and understanding as they progress through the levels. It is also essential that this understanding comes through the children's first hand experience. This should be achieved through a range of contexts to which the children can relate. We believe that these activities fulfil this criteria and the first chart (on pages 10 and 11) shows how an analysis of the activities can be matched to the Programmes of Study for science.

The relevant Statements of Attainment for both profile components which the children will experience are detailed in the teaching notes on the opposite page of each worksheet.

The charts overleaf give a breakdown of the activities matched to the Programmes of Study for Science (chart 1) and the Programmes of Study for Technology (chart 2).

An analysis of *Problem-Solving in Primary Science and Technology* against the National Curriculum Programmes of Study for Science for 5–11-year-olds.

	1 Which way now?	2 Round and about	3 A tangled web	4 A real fiddle	5 Just a minute	6 An alarming drip	7 Keeping cosy	8 Rock on, Tommy!	9 A grain of truth	10 Going down	11 Crafty raft	12 Rip a tissue	13 Up, up and away	14 The big lean	15 The power of the press	16 The brick
AT1 Exploration of Science	●	●	●	●	●	●	●	●	●	●	●	●	●	●	●	●
AT2 The Variety of Life																
AT3 Processes of Life																
AT4 Genetics and Evolution																
AT5 Human Influences on Earth																
AT6 Types & Uses of Materials					●	●	●	●	●	●	●	●	●	●	●	●
AT9 Earth and Atmosphere							●									
AT10 Forces					●			●		●	●	●	●	●	●	●
AT11 Electricity and Magnetism			●	●		●										
AT12 Information Technology					●											
AT13 Energy							●									
AT14 Sound and Music																
AT15 Using Light																
AT16 Earth in Space					●	●										

An analysis of *Problem-Solving in Primary Science and Technology* against the National Curriculum Programmes of Study for Technology for 5–11-year-olds.

	1 Which way now?	2 Round and about	3 A tangled web	4 A real fiddle	5 Just a minute	6 An alarming drip	7 Keeping cosy	8 Rock on, Tommy!	9 A grain of truth	10 Going down	11 Crafty raft	12 Rip a tissue	13 Up, up and away	14 The big lean	15 The power of the press	16 The brick
Developing and Using Artefacts, Systems and Environment	●	●	●	●	●	●	●	●	●	●	●	●	●	●	●	●
Working with Materials			●	●	●	●	●	●	●	●	●		●	●	●	●
Developing and Communicating Ideas					●	●					●	●	●	●	●	●
Satisfying Needs and Opportunities					●	●						●				
Information Technology Capability					●	●				●						

			●			●		●					●	17 Target practice
			●	●		●		●					●	18 A real drag
			●			●		●					●	19 Medieval misery
			●			●							●	20 Raise the drawbridge
						●	●	●					●	21 What a breeze
			●			●	●	●					●	22 The long drop
			●			●	●	●					●	23 The little twister
			●			●	●	●					●	24 Flight of fancy
			●	●		●							●	25 The jet machine
								●					●	26 A marble sorter
								●					●	27 Melanie the mixer
	●												●	28 A real smartie
	●												●	29 A fair cop
	●							●					●	30 A box of delights
●				●						●	●	●	●	31 Planetary puzzle
				●	●			●					●	32 The silver snatch
				●	●			●					●	33 Take care
				●	●	●		●	●				●	34 The pull
			●	●				●					●	35 Lunchtime scramble
			●	●				●			●		●	36 A cool carrier
			●	●				●					●	37 Radiator research
							●				●	●	●	38 Seedy solution
	●							●			●		●	39 Over the top
	●			●						●	●		●	40 Eyesight examination
	●										●		●	41 Funny faces
	●										●		●	42 Standing out
						●		●					●	43 The battle of the bags
						●		●			●		●	44 The crunch
						●		●					●	45 A sticky solution
							●	●					●	46 A teddy bear's picnic
						●		●			●		●	47 Scrambled egg
	●							●					●	48 Bubble trouble

	●	●	●	●	17 Target practice
●	●		●	●	18 A real drag
	●	●	●	●	19 Medieval misery
	●	●	●	●	20 Raise the drawbridge
			●	●	21 What a breeze
●	●	●	●	●	22 The long drop
●	●	●	●	●	23 The little twister
●	●	●	●	●	24 Flight of fancy
●		●	●	●	25 The jet machine
	●	●	●	●	26 A marble sorter
	●	●	●	●	27 Melanie the mixer
			●		28 A real smartie
		●	●	●	29 A fair cop
		●	●	●	30 A box of delights
●	●	●		●	31 Planetary puzzle
●	●	●	●	●	32 The silver snatch
●	●	●	●	●	33 Take care
●		●	●	●	34 The pull
●	●	●	●	●	35 Lunchtime scramble
●	●	●	●	●	36 A cool carrier
●	●	●		●	37 Radiator research
●	●	●		●	38 Seedy solution
	●	●	●	●	39 Over the top
●	●	●		●	40 Eyesight examination
		●	●	●	41 Funny faces
	●	●	●	●	42 Standing out
	●	●	●	●	43 The battle of the bags
	●	●			44 The crunch
	●		●	●	45 A sticky solution
	●	●	●	●	46 A teddy bear's picnic
	●		●	●	47 Scrambled egg
			●	●	48 Bubble trouble

The National Technology Curriculum

The Programmes of Study for Technology states that children should 'develop design and technology capability by exploring familiar situations' and 'look at familiar things . . . as starting points for some of their design activities.' The materials in the pack fulfil this criteria. Activities such as 'Melanie the Mixer' and 'The Battle of the Bags' provide children with familiar situations taken from their experiences to investigate and thus design and make artefacts which provide solutions. The activities also meet the requirements of the Programmes of Study for key stages 1 and 2 in that children are given opportunities of:

- Developing and using artefacts, systems and environments: making and controlling models, investigating different tools, powering vehicles, designing machines etc.
- Working with materials: modelling with pliable materials, glueing materials, choosing appropriate materials, using tools appropriately and safely.
- Developing and communicating ideas: drawing models, designing machines, taking measurements, sketching.
- Satisfying needs and addressing opportunities: sharing materials when working together, testing and evaluating their models, discussing how they could improve models.

5 How can I use this material effectively?

Using the material in the classroom

Approaches to science

The various approaches to the teaching of science and technology depend upon the experience and interests of the teacher and children, the age and background of the children and the resources available. This material can be adapted to any of the three main approaches experienced in the primary school:

- the thematic or topic approach
- the 'timetable slot for science' approach
- the 'science as it arises' approach.

Having chosen the approach which is the most suitable to you, the different aspects of organisation of the activities can be considered.

Grouping

The number of children within each group is clearly dependent upon the children's experience of co-operative groupwork. If the children have little experience, it is advantageous to work in pairs initially and gradually build up the numbers to four. It is important that all children feel they have a purpose within the group, and initially it may prove useful to outline specific tasks to each individual. Sorting and classifying-type activities encourage co-operation within a group (e.g. Challenge 30 *A box of delights*).

The number of groups working on the activities will depend on the availability of materials and the nature of the activities. Some activities which demand large amounts of constructional material are best used with only one or two groups within the class at any one time.

On the other hand, some of the activities (e.g. Challenge 24 *Flight of fancy*) may be presented to the whole class for discussion. The class can then divide into groups to develop and make their designs. The final stage involves the whole class testing and evaluating their models.

Positioning of groups within the classroom

Among the things to be considered are:

- the safety aspect – if children have to climb on chairs to test their parachutes, it is advisable to position them in a quiet area away from the general class movement.
- the noise level of an activity – any activity which involves sawing, hammering, etc. can be distracting to others and is best positioned to the sides or corners of the room.
- an avoidance of unnecessary movement – general equipment such as scissors, Sellotape and paper can be stored centrally in the classroom thus minimising movement.

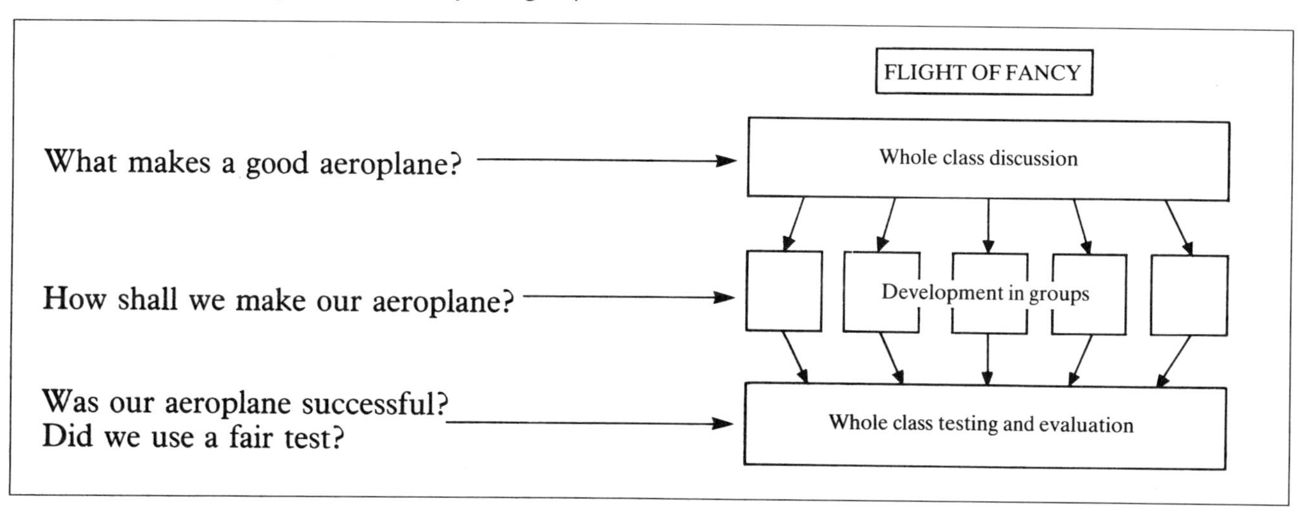

Speed and sequencing

- Some of the activities take longer to complete than others so it is essential that children know what to do on completion of the task.
- There may be a logical order to the tasks and children may become frustrated and lose interest if they are unable to see a solution because they have not completed a preliminary activity.
- If only part of the class is working on a particular activity which requires a significant amount of teacher attention the other children should have some other (preferably integrated) activity on which they can work profitably.

Communication

1 Between teacher and children

It is important to find the right balance between:

- instructional communication – so that the children are aware of exactly what the task is.
- information giving – and reminding the children of the value of researching the problem before starting.
- getting children's ideas – so that they not only value their own thoughts but appreciate the suggestions of others.
- clarifying understanding – which can avoid frustration and give children a clear sense of purpose.
- stimulating interest – a question at the appropriate time can bolster confidence and stimulate perseverance.

2 Child to child

Children learn much from each other and the sharing of ideas can stimulate children's creativity. The 'buzz' which occurs when children are engrossed in an activity not only helps them to clarify their own ideas, but also encourages them to recognise that other people's viewpoints are valuable and that by working and talking together a solution is made easier.

3 Between children and teacher

The discussion which is generated at the end of an activity is crucial. Children gain much by reporting back to both peers and teacher. By talking through their way of working they are clarifying and justifying their own solution and also gaining experience in sequencing skills, as well as improving their oral skills. If children are asked to comment on their enjoyment of the activities, they feel that their own opinions are valued and their self-esteem rises.

Recording

A common complaint from children is that if they have made a model, or been on a visit, they are routinely asked to write about it even if they see no purpose in it. For effective learning it is essential that the children see a purpose in any recording that you ask them to do.

Sometimes the finished product is seen by the child as an adequate record (e.g. Challenge 26 *A marble sorter*) but during the process some prototype solutions will need amending. It is useful to encourage children to make rough notes or diagrams of various 'prototypes' noting amendments as they proceed.

Some activities require the completion of tables (e.g. Challenge 42 *Standing out*). With less experienced children it may be necessary to produce a table which they just have to fill in, although older, more experienced children will enjoy the challenge of drawing up their own table.

A useful idea to consider is the 'group report' where children decide together how to present a joint record of their group's work; they will enjoy designing a poster or presenting a co-operative display in which each member of the group has played a part.

Children should be encouraged to record their findings in a wide variety of ways in order to widen their communication skills. All of the following are possible ways for children to record their findings:

- models
- talk
- written reports
- diagrams and pictures
- tables and graphs
- drama
- dance
- poetry
- photographs
- tape-recording
- video-recording
- using a computer, etc.

Resources

An essential feature of problem-solving is that it gives the responsibility of solving the problem to the children. The teacher is there not as a provider of answers but rather as a manager of materials and resources, and a consultant to guide children towards fruitful areas of research and possible solutions.

This latter role, which involves judging when to give advice, is vital. To give too little help can leave a group struggling and disheartened and remove any confidence that the group might have in solving future problems. To give too much help could take away much of the satisfaction children might feel upon successfully solving a problem.

Frequently, the best type of advice is to direct children towards available and appropriate resources to research possible solutions. These resources could include: library books, magazines, posters, video programmes, etc.

Research skills are an important aspect of problem-solving activities. It is not intended that children should produce solutions to the problems in isolation and unaided. The development of a set of resource materials, such as books and magazines, which is linked to each topic or theme, will go a long way to ensure the successful use of problem-solving materials.

The challenges in this pack are designed to use cheap and readily-available materials. Experience has shown that the following areas are good sources of materials:

- **shoe shops and supermarkets** for boxes and cardboard
- **dairies** for yoghurt pots
- **electrical and engineering firms** for wire and magnets
- **timber yards** for wood off-cuts
- **the local secondary school** for the loan of spirit thermometers, measuring cylinders, weighing machines, etc.
- **parents**, not only for the provision of materials but also to come into the classroom and help in the teaching situation. Do ensure that the helping parent is aware of the need to let the children pursue their own lines of enquiry and the importance of open-ended questioning. They may be too keen to do all the work for the children.

If all else fails, the following commercial suppliers have been found to be useful:

Roopers
20 Ridgewood Industrial Park
Uckfield
East Sussex TN22 5SX

Technology Teaching Systems Ltd
Penmore House
Hasland Road
Hasland
Chesterfield S41 0SJ

Surplus Buying Agency
Woodburn Road School
Woodburn Road
Sheffield S9 3LQ
(send SAE for stock list)

Philip Harris Ltd
Lynn Lane
Shenstone
Lichfield
Staffordshire SW14 0EE

Safety

In any teaching situation the safety of the children is of paramount importance and a key responsibility of the teacher in the classroom. Open-ended investigations, where children are planning their own procedures, need careful supervision and teachers must insist that any planned procedure is checked before children are allowed to carry it out. If certain stages in the procedure could cause safety problems, children need to be guided towards an alternative approach.

It is essential to develop in children a sense of care and respect for the equipment and materials they might use. A responsibility for maintaining tidiness throughout the lesson should be encouraged in the children. They will respond well to these expectations providing adequate time is set aside for tidying up.

Careful choice of equipment and materials can help in reducing any safety problems. For example:

- use plastic beakers and measuring cylinders rather than glass ones.
- use clearly scaled spirit thermometers. Do **not** use mercury thermometers as the liquid mercury, when spilt from a broken thermometer, is a serious health hazard to children.
- use hot water from a kettle with care, but never use very hot or near boiling water. Supervise or carry out the pouring of hot water as appropriate and keep hot kettles well away from the children.
- only use naked flames, such as candles, under very close supervision. Children with long hair should have it tied back and loose cuffs should be rolled up. Ensure a fire bucket or sand bucket is nearby.
- do not use hot glue guns. If glue guns are felt to be necessary the type which delivers glue under pressure is much safer.
- use water-based glues rather than the solvent or rubber-based glues. A water-based wood glue such as PVA is clean and safe to use.
- do not use any chemical salts such as copper sulphate and cobalt chloride. These are poisonous if swallowed.

Below is a photocopiable list for children which can make the classroom a safer working area.

Safety Rules

1 Keep your work areas tidy.

2 Clean up any mess quickly.

3 Keep bags and clutter away from the work areas.

4 Check that everyone in your group is working safely.

5 If in doubt, ask your teacher.

6 The activities in detail

In this section there are 48 worksheets designed to be used as Master copies for photocopying. There is no restriction on their duplication within the purchaser's establishment.

The opposite page of each worksheet contains all the relevant information needed to use that activity in the primary classroom.

Which way now?

Tom has overslept again!
He's got three minutes to get to school.

Guess which is the shortest way.

Test your guess as carefully as you can.

Challenge 1: Which way now?

Specific aims:

To develop skills in predicting.
To develop skills in planning investigations.
To develop skills in measuring.
To develop skills in manipulating.

Equipment per group:

- centimetre ruler
- 2p coin or plastic substitute
- Blu-Tack or Plasticine
- cotton thread
- thin string
- Sellotape
- scissors

Notes

An important aspect of this challenge is that children predict which is the shortest route before they actually attempt to measure the length of the different routes.

There are a number of solutions to the problem. The one used most frequently is to place some cotton thread along each route in turn and then compare the lengths. Blu-Tack, Plasticine or Sellotape can be used to hold the thread in place. This method allows younger children, who are not used to the units of length, to tackle the problem by simply comparing the lengths of their cotton threads.

Another solution is to use the coin as a measuring wheel. Children measure the circumference of the coin by carefully rolling it along the graduated ruler. The coin is then rolled along the route counting the number of revolutions. An incomplete revolution can be measured with the ruler.

This challenge can be extended to other mapping activities, such as looking at maps of the local area and measuring the distances between certain points. It is also an excellent introductory exercise for a topic on 'Road safety'.

Key vocabulary

guess

National Science Curriculum analysis

Attainment target	Statements of Attainment
1	2a, 2b, 2c, 2d, 2e 3a, 3d, 3e, 3f 4a, 4i

National Technology Curriculum analysis

Attainment target	Statements of Attainment
1	1a, 1b, 3a
3	1a, 2a, 3b, 3d
4	1a, 2a, 3a, 3b

Round and about

A challenge:
Measure around Tom's profile using the ruler and a 2p coin.

Work carefully to give an accurate answer.

Challenge 2: Round and about

Specific aims:

To develop skills in measuring.
To develop skills in planning investigations.
To develop skills in manipulating.

Equipment per group:

- centimetre ruler
- coin or plastic substitute
- cotton thread or string (optional)

Notes

The limited equipment provided with this challenge forces children towards using the coin as a measuring wheel. Younger children can work to the nearest centimetre, while older children might be expected to work toward the nearest millimetre.

Some children first put the coin down flat on the outline and use the coin's diameter as a measure of length. This leads to inaccuracies with the sharply curved parts of the line.

One problem noted during the trialling of this challenge is that the coin slips as it is rolled along the line. One solution is to carefully wrap the coin in Sellotape with the sticky surface outwards, then with careful manipulation accurate results can be obtained.

For younger children with less experience who need more practice in measurement and manipulation, it would be beneficial to provide string or thread as well as the coin. This additional equipment gives the children another possible solution (see Challenge 1 *Which way now?*) and will allow them to complete the activity without frustration. As an extension exercise children can compare the different methods from the point of view of accuracy and ease of use.

The principle of the measuring wheel seen in this challenge is used widely in everyday life with such things as milometers on bicycles and cars, map measuring wheels, road engineers' measuring wheels, etc.

Key vocabulary

circumference, profile

National Science Curriculum analysis

Attainment target	Statements of Attainment
1	3c, 3d, 3e 4e, 4i

National Technology Curriculum analysis

Attainment target	Statements of Attainment
1	3a
3	3b, 3d
4	3a, 3b

A tangled web

A challenge:
You have:
- an empty cotton reel,
- a 30 centimetre ruler,
- exactly 10 metres of tangled cotton thread.

Use these to find out how many times your thread will go around the cotton reel.

Remember: Think before you do anything.

Challenge 3: A tangled web

Specific aims:
To develop skills in measuring.
To develop skills in planning investigations.
To develop skills in manipulating.

Equipment per group:
- centimetre ruler
- cotton reel
- 10 metre length (approximately) of tangled cotton thread
- calculator

Notes
This problem does **not** involve the untangling of the cotton thread. A common approach is to measure the circumference of the cotton reel by wrapping a loose end of the thread around the cotton reel. This length, equal to the circumference, can be measured with the centimetre ruler. The children have been told that the length of the thread is 10 metres and so they can calculate the number of turns the tangled thread can make around the reel.

For many children, a calculator is a valuable tool in this investigation. Able children may realise that a more accurate result can be achieved by wrapping the thread three or four times around the reel to find the average circumference.

N.B. Empty cotton reels can be bought in bulk from most large educational suppliers. See the section on *Resources* for a list of addresses.

There are many common features in Challenges 1, 2 and 3. One successful approach is to use all three activities with different groups within one class. The spread of activity across the groups minimises children copying the 'answer' from their neighbouring group.

Key vocabulary
calculate, circumference, tangled

National Science Curriculum analysis

Attainment target	Statements of Attainment
1	3c, 3d, 3e 4e, 4i
12	2b, 3b

National Technology Curriculum analysis

Attainment target	Statements of Attainment
1	4a, 4e
2	4a
3	4b, 4d
4	4a

A real fiddle

A challenge:
How thick is your piece of string?

Think first!

Work carefully to give an accurate answer.

Challenge 4: A real fiddle

Special aims:

To develop skills in measuring.
To develop skills in planning investigations.
To develop skills in manipulating.

Equipment per group:

- string
- centimetre ruler
- pencil
- scissors
- Sellotape
- magnifying lens
- calculator

Notes

Most solutions use the principle of measuring many thicknesses of string and then calculating the thickness of a single length of string.

One approach involves neatly coiling the string round a pencil and measuring the thickness of the coil (containing, say, 10 turns). A more elegant version of this solution involves wrapping the string directly round the ruler.

Another version involves Sellotaping short lengths of string side by side onto a piece of paper and again measuring the thickness of, say, 10 lengths.

For many children a calculator is a valuable tool in this investigation.

The degree of difficulty with this problem can be controlled by using different thicknesses of string. Thick string is much easier to work with than thin string, but it must never be so thick that an accurate direct reading can be made from one thickness.

This activity can be extended to find the thickness of a single sheet of paper or the thickness of a human hair.

Key vocabulary

coil, fiddly, magnify, thick, thickness

National Science Curriculum analysis

Attainment target	Statements of Attainment
1	3c, 3d, 3e 4e, 4i
12	2b, 3b

National Technology Curriculum analysis

Attainment target	Statements of Attainment
1	4a
2	4a
4	4a

Just a minute

A challenge:
Design and make a timer.
Your timer must measure accurately an interval of 1 minute.

Challenge 5: Just a minute

Specific aims:

To develop skills in measuring.
To develop skills in designing and making.

Equipment per group:

- thin candle or wax taper
- flat dish to hold the candle
- felt pen
- pins
- table fork
- clean dry sand or salt
- digital stop-watch
- assorted plastic containers, e.g. yoghurt pots, washing-up bottles, lemonade bottles, etc.
- scissors
- matches (to be held by the teacher)

Notes

This is an open-ended problem with many possible solutions. A limiting factor to the range of solutions produced is the variety of material available. If children are given the chance to think about the problem at home, they can bring in some of the equipment themselves.

If care and patience are exercised with this problem, the results can be remarkably accurate.

Some noted solutions are as follows:

1. using the wax taper as a candle clock, having calibrated the rate of burning against the stop-watch.
2. using the yoghurt pot and sand to make a simple 'egg timer'.
3. using a plastic container punctured with a small hole and calibrated to empty a certain volume of water in the required time.
4. using a fork stuck in the side of a candle designed to fall out as the candle burns down.

If a group of children choose to use the candle or taper, the usual safety procedures must apply, with long hair tied back and cuffs fastened.

If a group of children choose to make a water clock they need to be placed near a sink.

The challenge can be extended using Challenge 6 *An alarming drip* and can form part of a broader theme on 'Time'.

Key vocabulary

interval, timer, wax taper

National Science Curriculum analysis

Attainment target	Statements of Attainment
1	2a, 2c, 2e 3c, 3d, 3e, 3i 4a, 4b, 4d, 4g, 4j
6	2a, 3b, 4d
10	3a, 3b, 4c
12	2b
16	2a, 2b

National Technology Curriculum analysis

Attainment target	Statements of Attainment
1	3a, 3b, 4e, 4f
2	3a, 3b, 3e, 4a, 4b
3	3a, 3b, 3d, 4a, 4b
4	3a, 3b, 4a

An alarming drip

A challenge:
Design and make a timer which sets off an alarm after 2 minutes. Make your timer as accurate as you can.

Challenge 6: An alarming drip

Specific aims:

To develop skills in measuring.
To develop skills in designing and making.

Equipment per group:

- as for Challenge 5, plus
- 2 batteries
- 6 connecting wires with crocodile clips
- low voltage buzzer
- ping-pong ball (or polystyrene spheres)
- drawing pins
- Sellotape

Safety note:

Remind children of the dangers of mains electricity and emphasise that in this exercise they are using 'safe' batteries and bulbs. They must not go home and investigate the mains supply.

Notes

This is an extension of Challenge 5 *Just a minute* and needs careful planning of the organisation of the equipment. Asking children to think about the problem and then bring in their own material from home makes the organisation considerably easier. It has proved beneficial to have only one or two groups doing this activity at any one time.

Most popular solutions involve water clocks and an electric buzzer circuit. One example is illustrated below.

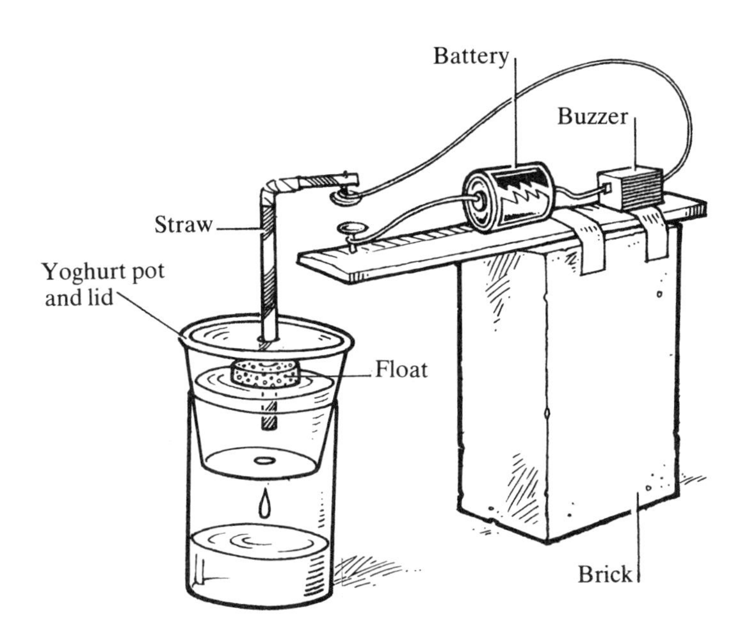

The water container acts as a water clock, the water level slowly falling as the water drips away. The float follows the falling water level allowing the drawing pin, attached to the straw, to move nearer to the fixed drawing pin. Eventually contact is made and the buzzer is activated.

This challenge links into work on 'Electricity' and unless this topic has already been introduced, children will need help in setting up the circuit.

Key vocabulary

alarm, buzzer, circuit, contact, crocodile clips, voltage

National Science Curriculum analysis

Attainment target	Statements of Attainment
1	4a, 4b, 4c, 4d, 4e, 4g
6	2a, 3b, 4d
11	3a, 3b, 4a, 5a

National Technology Curriculum analysis

Attainment target	Statements of Attainment
1	4e, 4f
2	4a, 4b
3	4a, 4b
4	4a

Keeping cosy

A challenge:
Is it true that large penguins can keep warmer than small penguins?

Investigate this idea using plastic bottles of different sizes.

Challenge 7: Keeping cosy

Specific aims:

To develop skills in measuring.
To develop skills in planning investigations.
To develop an appreciation of the problems of small animals in cold climates.

Equipment per group:

- kettle/source of hot water
- spirit thermometer
- assorted plastic bottles of various sizes but of similar shape
- digital stop-clock

Safety note:

Remind children to be careful near hot water. Do not use boiling water.

Notes

This investigation is a good example of using models to test a hypothesis or idea.

The usual solution is to use three similar-shaped plastic bottles of differing size to represent a large, a medium-sized and a small penguin. Each bottle is filled with hot water at the same temperature and the fall in temperature over a given time is noted for each 'penguin'.

Younger children will need the hot water poured out for them. They may also like to decorate the bottles and make them more 'penguin-like'.

To ease any equipment problems, children can be asked to bring in empty plastic containers such as shampoo bottles, drinks bottles and washing-up liquid bottles. From the range collected, sets of three can be selected, the bottles in each set being of similar shape but a variety of sizes.

This investigation can be extended to look at the problems of keeping premature babies warm in hospitals. Children can also investigate the insulating properties of materials such as fur and feathers by glueing them to similar-sized containers and then comparing how quickly their temperatures fall.

A typical question is:
'Will an animal covered in fur be as warm as an animal of the same size covered in feathers?'

Key vocabulary

cooling, insulation, temperature, thermometer

National Science Curriculum analysis

Attainment target	Statements of Attainment
1	2a, 2b, 2c, 2d, 2e, 2f 3a, 3b, 3c, 3d, 3e, 3f, 3g 4a, 4b, 4c, 4d, 4e, 4g, 4h, 4i
6	4d
9	2b
13	2a, 3b, 4d

National Technology Curriculum analysis

Attainment target	Statements of Attainment
1	2a, 2b, 3b, 4e
2	3a, 3d, 4a
3	2a, 2b, 3d, 4b
4	2a, 3a, 3b

Rock on, Tommy!

A challenge:
Measure accurately the volume of your lump of rock salt.

Think before you start!

Challenge 8: Rock on, Tommy!

Specific aims:

To develop skills in measuring.
To develop skills in planning investigations.
To develop an appreciation of the concept of solubility.

Equipment per group:

- clingfilm
- thin plastic bag
- measuring cylinder
- cotton thread
- lump of rock salt
- paint brush
- small tin of gloss paint or bottle of nail varnish
- assorted yoghurt pots

Notes

The usual solution to measuring the volume of an irregular shape, such as a rock, is to carefully lower it into a container brimming with water. The rock will displace a volume of water equal to its own volume. This water can be collected and its volume read in a measuring cylinder. Using the lump of rock salt, the problem is slightly more difficult, as the salt will dissolve slowly into the water.

A widely used solution is to cover the rock salt in clingfilm or a plastic bag and then measure its volume by the displacement of water.

Another, less elegant method, is to paint the rock salt with a waterproof paint and again, when dry, measure its volume by the displacement of water.

An alternative activity, which is more relevant to the children's everyday life, is to ask them to measure the volume of a slightly damaged sugar cube. A broken corner will prevent them calculating the sugar lump's volume as if it were a regular cube. In this modified version, the volume involved will be small, demanding more precision from the children.

Key vocabulary

dissolve, lump, measuring cylinder, volume

National Science Curriculum analysis

Attainment target	Statements of Attainment
1	4a, 4b, 4c, 4d
6	4a, 4c
10	3b

National Technology Curriculum analysis

Attainment target	Statements of Attainment
1	4e
2	4a, 4b, 4d
3	4b
4	4a, 4b

A grain of truth

A challenge:
How heavy is 1 grain of rice?

Challenge 9: A grain of truth

Specific aims:

To develop skills in measuring.
To develop skills in planning investigations.

Equipment per group:

- digital weighing machine
- approximately 50 g rice
- calculator

Notes

The usual solution to this problem is to weigh out accurately, say, 20 g of rice and count the number of rice grains in this mass of rice. From these two figures the average mass of one grain of rice can be calculated. Children do not find the mathematics of the problem easy and a calculator is very useful at this point.

The problem can be extended to look at the mass of apples, potatoes, sweets, etc., developing the idea that a larger sample leads to greater accuracy in the situation where individual objects are not identical.

The challenge can be used as part of a topic based on 'Food'.

Key vocabulary

accurate, average, calculate, grain, sample

National Science Curriculum analysis

Attainment target	Statements of Attainment
1	3a, 3c, 3d, 3e, 3f, 3g, 3i 4a, 4b, 4c, 4d, 4e, 4h, 4i, 4j
6	4c

National Technology Curriculum analysis

Attainment target	Statements of Attainment
2	4a, 4b, 4c
3	4b, 4c

Going down

The shape of their bodies is important to animals which live in water. Some shapes make moving through water very easy.

A challenge:
You have 2 pieces of Plasticine, each weighing 5 grams.

By changing their shape:

1 Make 1 piece fall through the water as quickly as you can.
2 Make the other piece fall through the water as slowly as you can.

You are not allowed to change the weight of the Plasticine pieces.

Challenge 10: Going down

Specific aims:
To develop skills in measuring.
To develop skills in planning investigations.
To develop skills in designing and making.
To develop an appreciation of the concept of streamlining.

Equipment per group:
- large, tall measuring cylinder
- two 5 g pieces of Plasticine (plus spares)
- large bowl
- digital stop-watch
- floor mop and bucket
- digital weighing machine (if available)
- wallpaper paste (optional)

Notes
This challenge is very useful for developing the concepts and skills of fair testing. Children need to be gently questioned to develop a fair test, i.e. the Plasticine shapes must always be released from the same position, and timing should take place between the same two points.

Unless a tall measuring cylinder is used, the intervals of time taken by the Plasticine shapes to fall can be very short and therefore difficult for the children to measure. An alternative approach is to replace the water in the measuring cylinder with dilute wallpaper paste. This slows the movement of the shapes considerably, making timing easier.

This activity also highlights the need to use multiple readings to give an average, rather than accepting the result of a single reading.

Most children have little difficulty in producing a streamlined shape, but have more difficulty in producing the slowly falling shape. Children are often tempted to alter the mass of the Plasticine ball and they need to be reminded that this is not allowed.

To reduce spillage of water, the measuring cylinder can be placed in a large bowl.

This challenge has been used successfully as part of a topic on 'Movement'.

Key vocabulary
average, shape, streamlined

National Science Curriculum analysis

Attainment target	Statements of Attainment
1	4a, 4b, 4c, 4d, 4e, 4h, 4i, 4j
6	3a, 3b, 4a, 4c
10	3b, 4a, 5a

National Technology Curriculum analysis

Attainment target	Statements of Attainment
2	4a
3	4b, 4d

Crafty raft

A challenge:
Using a 10 cm square of cooking foil, make a craft which can carry the greatest load.

Test your craft.

Then try to improve it to carry an even greater load.

Challenge 11: Crafty raft

Specific aims:

To develop skills in designing and making.
To develop an appreciation of the concept of floating and sinking.

Equipment per group:

- 10 cm square of cooking foil (plus spares)
- scissors
- large bowl or bucket
- Sellotape
- assorted 5 g, 10 g, and 20 g masses
- floor mop and bucket
- box of centicubes

Notes

Children need to be encouraged to design and make a wide variety of craft and to test each one in turn. Have plenty of spare foil squares handy.

Remind children that the aim of the exercise is to produce not a replica of the craft on the workcard but a craft which floats and can carry most weight.

The load carried by many foil craft is surprisingly high and can be given greater impact if centicubes are used to test the craft rather than metal masses.

A complementary problem is to provide children with a known mass of Plasticine and ask them to design and make a Plasticine craft capable of carrying the greatest load. They are allowed to use only the fixed mass of Plasticine. The essential design feature is to have a very thin-walled vessel with a wide bottom for stability. The contrast between this craft carrying a large load of centicubes and a ball of Plasticine which sinks is dramatic.

These two investigations have been used successfully as part of a topic on 'Movement'.

Key vocabulary

aluminium, craft, float, foil, raft, sink

National Science Curriculum analysis

Attainment target	Statements of Attainment
1	3a, 3c, 3d, 3f, 3g, 3h, 3i 4a, 4b, 4c, 4d, 4h, 4i, 4j
6	3b, 4a
10	3b

National Technology Curriculum analysis

Attainment target	Statements of Attainment
2	3b, 3e, 4a
3	3d, 4b, 4d
4	3b

Rip a tissue

Paper tissues vary in price and quality.

Two challenges:

1 Find out which tissue is the strongest when wet.

2 Find out which tissue will soak up the most water.

Challenge 12: Rip a tissue

Specific aims:
To develop skills in measuring.
To develop skills in planning investigations.

Equipment per group:
- assorted paper tissues (the wider the range the better)
- kitchen roll
- paper towels
- Plasticine or Blu-Tack
- assorted 5 g and 10 g masses
- digital weighing machine
- assorted yoghurt pots
- Sellotape

Notes
This is a very open-ended investigation and it is recommended that a group concentrate on one of the challenges, rather than tackle both.

To ease problems of classroom organisation, a group of children can be given the problem and asked to plan their investigation. They can then provide the teacher with an outline plan and a list of the required equipment.

There are a number of successful approaches to each of these challenges.

One approach to the first activity involves carefully adding small masses to a wet tissue which has been stretched across a yoghurt pot. The idea of 'fair testing' needs to be emphasised by the teacher.

One approach to the second activity involves weighing different sodden tissues after the excess water has been allowed to drip away. The sodden tissues need to be weighed in a container to protect the weighing machine. In this situation, using the 'TARE' button fitted to most weighing machines makes the operation more straightforward for younger children.

Using a range of tissues including kitchen roll and paper towels forces children to consider how to make their test fair, when the tissues can be of different sizes and thicknesses. Many groups cut their tissues to a standard size for testing while others, more accurately, test a standard mass of tissue paper.

This work can be extended to look at other aspects of paper tissues, e.g. value for money and comfort. The challenges have also been used as part of a topic on 'Water'.

Key vocabulary
absorb, soak up, strongest

National Science Curriculum analysis

Attainment target	Statements of Attainment
1	3a, 3c, 3d, 3e, 3f, 3g, 3h, 3i 4a, 4b, 4c, 4d, 4e, 4h, 4i, 4j
6	3a, 3b, 4a, 4b, 4c
10	3a, 3b, 4a

National Technology Curriculum analysis

Attainment target	Statements of Attainment
1	3a
3	3a, 3d, 4b
4	3a, 3b

Up, up and away

A challenge:
Design and make a tower using 25 drinking straws and 1 metre of Sellotape. Your tower must support a marble as high as possible.

Your tower must be able to support the marble for at least **30 seconds.**

Challenge 13: Up, up and away

Specific aims:

To develop skills in planning investigations.
To develop skills in designing and making.
To develop an appreciation of the concept of a triangular shape being 'strong'.

Equipment per group:

- 25 drinking straws
- 1 metre of Sellotape
- 1 marble
- digital stop-watch

Notes

In this challenge it is essential to use **only** the specified materials. This restriction ensures that children plan their construction carefully. The limitation on Sellotape prevents them from wrapping up the structure in half a roll of tape!

In trials this problem proved extremely popular, with towers of 50 cm and over being built by quite young children. The testing stage can be exciting as the tower sways under the weight of the marble and the clock ticks slowly towards the 30 second mark.

Challenges 13, 14 and 15 form a group of investigations which fit well into topics on 'Buildings', 'Structures' or 'Forces'. The use of all three exercises with different groups within a class minimises the copying of ideas and designs, and can lead to some very imaginative work.

Key vocabulary

force, structure, support, sway, tower, triangular

National Science Curriculum analysis

Attainment target	Statements of Attainment
1	2a, 2c, 2d, 2e, 2f 3a, 3d, 3e, 3h, 3i 4a, 4b
6	4a, 4b
10	3a, 4a, 5a, 5b

National Technology Curriculum analysis

Attainment target	Statements of Attainment
2	3b
3	1a, 2a, 3a, 3d, 4a, 4b
4	1a, 2a, 3b

The big lean

A challenge:
Design and make a structure using 25 wooden spills and 1 metre of Sellotape. Your structure must support a marble as far out from the table as possible.

Your structure must not come in contact with the floor or any of the other furniture in the room. It must support the marble for at least 30 seconds.

Challenge 14: The big lean

Specific aims:
To develop skills in planning investigations.
To develop skills in designing and making.
To develop an appreciation of the concept of a triangular shape being 'strong'.

Equipment per group:
- 25 wooden spills
- 1 metre of Sellotape
- 1 marble
- digital stop-watch

Notes
The wooden spills are available from newsagents and hardware shops. However, drinking straws can be substituted if the spills are unobtainable. As in Challenge 13 *Up, up and away*, the limitation of materials is an excellent way to ensure that children design their structure carefully before they build it.

Many first attempts are not completely successful, and children need to be given time to re-think and re-design their structures. Although time-consuming, this is a valuable learning experience and is well worth the commitment.

Younger children have found it necessary to Sellotape the base of the structure to the table or desk, but to make the activity more challenging for older children, the emphasis should be placed on the structure being free-standing.

Key vocabulary
force, spills, splints, structure, support, sway, tower, triangular

National Science Curriculum analysis

Attainment target	Statements of Attainment
1	2a, 2c, 2d, 2e, 2f 3a, 3d, 3e, 3h, 3i 4a, 4b
6	4a, 4b
10	3a, 4a, 5a, 5b

National Technology Curriculum analysis

Attainment target	Statements of Attainment
2	3b
3	1a, 2a, 3a, 3d, 4a, 4b
4	1a, 2a, 3b

The power of the press

A challenge:
Design and build a bridge across a gap of 1 metre, using only 1 newspaper and 1 metre of Sellotape.

Test your bridge.

Then try to make your bridge stronger.

Challenge 15: The power of the press

Specific aims:

To develop skills in planning investigations.
To develop skills in designing and making.
To develop different ideas on making paper stronger.

Equipment per group:

- 1 tabloid newspaper
- 1 metre of Sellotape
- assorted masses (to test the bridge's strength)

Safety note:

Warn children of the danger to toes of falling weights.

Notes

Using tabloid newspapers makes the problem more challenging as individual sheets are not long enough to span the one metre gap.

One widely used solution is to roll the sheets of newspaper into long tubes and then lay them side by side. Another solution is to strengthen the sheets of newspaper by folding them into 'concertina' shapes and then taping these strengthened sheets of paper together to make the bridge. The folded concertinas are surprisingly strong when used 'edge on' to support the masses.

As an extension of Challenges 13, 14 and 15, commercial construction kits such as Meccano, LEGO and Somertech could be used to make more elaborate structures, the span being scaled down to suit the building materials.

The topic can also be extended to look at the variety of bridges which exist either in the locality or nationally.

Key vocabulary

bridge, force, load, span, structure

National Science Curriculum analysis

Attainment target	Statements of Attainment
1	2a, 2c, 2d, 2e, 2f 3a, 3c, 3d, 3e, 3f, 3g, 3h, 3i 4a, 4b, 4g, 4h, 4i, 4j
6	4a, 4b
10	3a, 4a, 5a, 5b

National Technology Curriculum analysis

Attainment target	Statements of Attainment
2	3b
3	2a, 3a, 3d, 4a, 4b
4	2a, 3b

The brick

For thousands of years people have tried to move heavy objects such as rocks and trees. Some of the ideas have been good and have made moving heavy things easier.

A challenge:
Design and make as many different devices as possible to move the brick.

Take care!
Mind your toes!

Challenge 16: The brick

Specific aims:

To develop skills in planning investigations.
To develop skills in designing and making.
To enable children to understand how a simple machine can make the moving of objects easier.

Equipment per group:

- 1 house brick
- string
- masses, e.g. 50 g, 100 g, 250 g
- pencils
- marbles
- tin lid (or similar)
- wheels
- cotton reels
- cardboard or 'Corriflute' sheets

Safety note:

Warn children to take care not to drop the brick on their toes.

Notes

There are a number of possible solutions to the challenge including the following:

1 using the pencils as rollers under the brick
2 placing the marbles under the tin lid, the brick on the tin lid and then rolling the brick along
3 setting up a slope down which the brick can slide
4 making a simple chassis fitted with wheels to carry the brick.

Younger children are happy to simply fasten string to the brick and then pull it over the rollers or marbles. Older children can extend the idea to use a pulley system.

An extension to this challenge which has proved popular is to replace the brick with a matchbox. Using the matchbox the challenge can be modified, for instance, to move the matchbox across a table, but to make it stop as near to the edge as possible. Another version is to find the fastest time to move the brick or matchbox along a fixed distance.

All the challenges mentioned can be fitted into a topic on 'Movement' and link in well with projects on the history of transport.

Key vocabulary

device, force, friction, rollers, slide

National Science Curriculum analysis

Attainment target	Statements of Attainment
1	1a, 1b 2a, 2c, 2d, 2e 3a, 3d, 3e, 3h, 3i 4a, 4b, 4g, 4i, 4j
10	1a, 2a, 3a, 4b, 4d

National Technology Curriculum analysis

Attainment target	Statements of Attainment
1	1b, 2a, 3a, 3b
3	1a, 2a, 2b, 3d, 4d
4	1a, 2a, 2b, 3a, 3b, 4c

Target practice

A challenge:
Design and make an elastic-powered device that can slide a coin on to a target 1 metre away.

How accurate can you make it?

If you put scores on the target, who can score the highest?

Challenge 17: Target practice

Specific aims:
To develop skills in planning investigations.
To develop skills in designing and making.

Equipment per group:
- card
- square section wood (1 cm × 1 cm)
- wood glue
- string
- scissors
- drawing pins
- elastic bands (assorted)
- coin or metal washer
- chalk (to mark out target)
- metre ruler
- cardboard tube
- Sellotape
- Plasticine or Blu-Tack
- paper clips
- stapler
- G clamps (if available)

Notes
The success of this activity depends on the availability of a wide variety of materials. One idea used successfully is to build up a collection of materials in a junk box which can then be used for this type of exercise. Again, children can be set the design problem to discuss in groups and asked to bring in suitable materials from home.

The problem can be made easier or more difficult by varying the size of the target and its distance from the launcher.

One solution is to make a simple V-frame as shown:

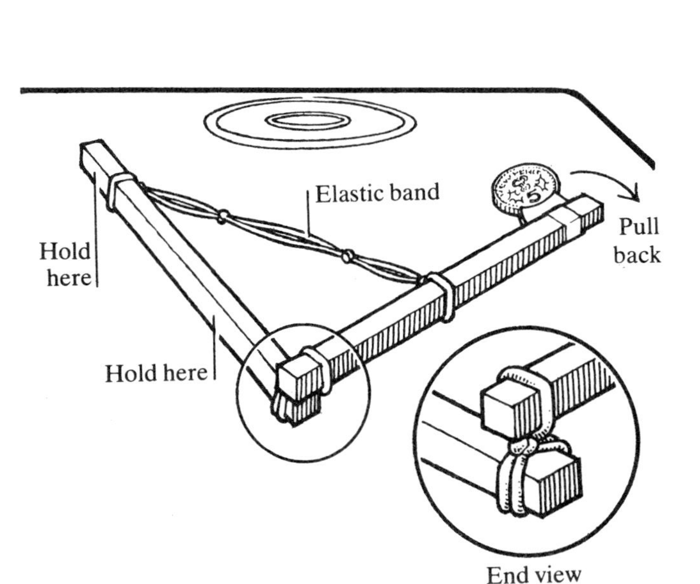

The structure is held flat against the table top and one arm tensioned against the elastic band. By trial and error, the position of the arm can be calibrated to slide the coin a certain distance. With practice, accuracy can be developed.

Key vocabulary
accurate, design, device, elastic, force, friction, launcher, target, tension

National Science Curriculum analysis

Attainment target	Statements of Attainment
1	2a, 2c, 2d, 2e 3a, 3c, 3e, 3h, 3i 4a, 4c, 4d, 4g, 4i, 4j
6	2a, 4a, 4b
10	2a, 3a, 4a, 4b, 4c
13	2b, 3c, 4c

National Technology Curriculum analysis

Attainment target	Statements of Attainment
2	2a, 3a, 3b, 3d, 4a, 4d
3	2a, 2b, 2c, 3c, 3d, 4b, 4d
4	2a, 2b, 3b, 4a, 4c

A real drag

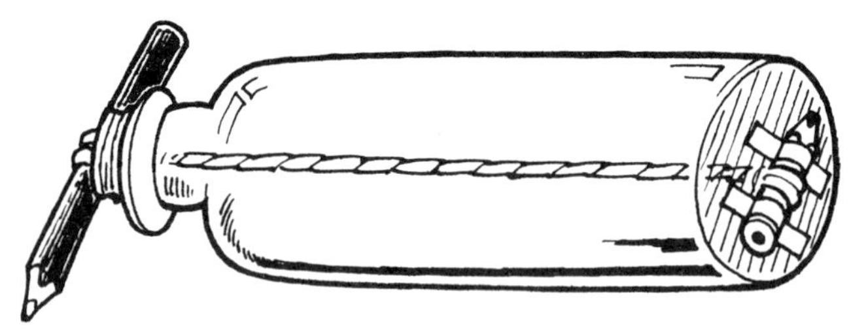

In this plan, a plastic soft-drinks bottle is used to make a model 'dragster'.
Its source of energy is a wound-up elastic band.

A challenge:
Without changing the elastic band, develop your machine to travel along a straight 3 metre course in the shortest time.

Challenge 18: A real drag

Specific aims:
To develop skills in designing and making.
To develop skills in measuring.

Equipment per group:
- plastic bottle (1.5 litre)
- elastic bands (assorted but including 5 thick ones for the drive elastic)
- pencils (one long, one short)
- Sellotape
- card
- digital stop-watch
- string

Notes
Children need some guidance in constructing a device made from a lemonade bottle using the plan. The drive elastic used can be made by knotting together, end to end, five thick elastic bands. In trials it proved best to pre-drill the bottle to take the drive elastic. A useful technique for threading the drive elastic through the bottle is to tie a length of string to one end of the elastic and pull the drive elastic into position using the string. It is best to tape the short pencil to the base of the bottle to ensure only the long pencil is free to rotate.

When the devices are tested, two problems need to be overcome by the children:
1 When the drive elastic is wound really tightly, the bottle skids across the floor, i.e. it produces wheel-spin. Children need to modify the bottle to grip the floor better. The usual solution is to wrap elastic bands round the bottle.
2 The bottle will veer to one side because the drive is only on one side. To overcome this, the usual solution is to build up one side with thick elastic bands and card. The problem can be made more difficult by making the course narrow. Conversely, a wide course produces fewer failures.

This challenge is a good opportunity to reinforce the idea that multiple readings are more accurate when averaged than one single timed run.

Key vocabulary
accurate, average, dragster, force, friction, grip, veer, wheel-spin

National Science Curriculum analysis

Attainment target	Statements of Attainment
1	3a, 3c, 3d, 3e, 3h, 3i 4a, 4b, 4c, 4d, 4i, 4j
6	4a, 4b
10	3a, 4a, 4b
12	3a
13	3a, 3c, 4c

National Technology Curriculum analysis

Attainment target	Statements of Attainment
2	4a, 4b, 4d
3	4b, 4d
4	4a, 4b

Medieval misery

In medieval times, catapults were used to hurl rocks and burning missiles at an enemy.

A challenge:
Design and make an elastic-powered catapult using the parts from a LEGO Technic 1 kit.

Your machine must be able to throw a 5 gram piece of Plasticine into a bucket 1 metre away.
It must be strong enough to withstand 3 firings without breaking.

Challenge 19: Medieval misery

Specific aims:

To develop skills in designing and making.
To develop skills in planning investigations.

Equipment per group:

- LEGO Technic 1 kit
- 5 g piece of Plasticine (plus spares)
- bucket/bowl
- metre ruler

Notes

If children have not used the LEGO kits before, they need time to become familiar with the different parts of the kit, and how they can be used. Once children are confident about using the LEGO kit their progress is remarkably quick.

Children produce a wide variety of designs, the two major stumbling blocks being accuracy and strength.

One of the simpler solutions is shown below:

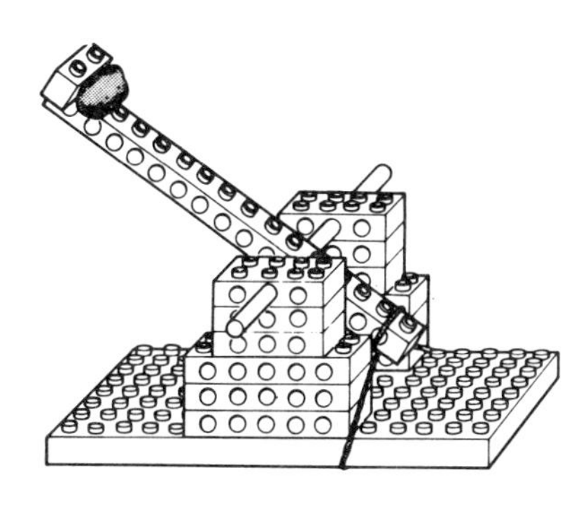

However, this design must be strengthened with additional pieces to withstand three consecutive firings.

A more sophisticated solution is based on a triangular frame shown on Activity card 3 (1031) in the LEGO Technic 1 kit.

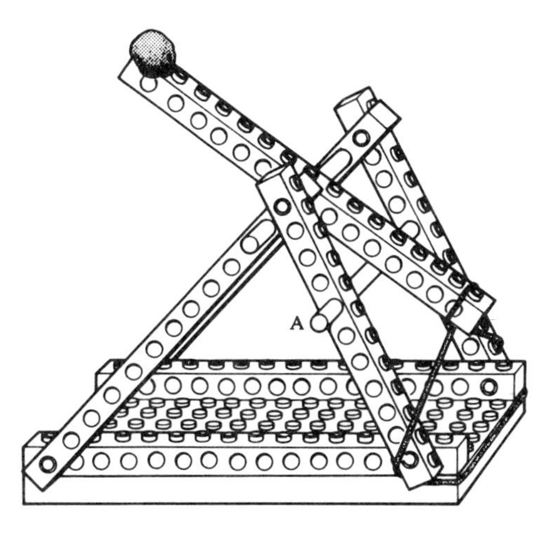

This structure needs no strengthening. An axle placed through the front legs at position A checks the movement of the arm after release, causing the Plasticine ball to separate from the arm at a particular point in the arc of the arm. The position of the axle can be adjusted to affect the aim of the catapult.

An alternative approach is to set the same challenge using materials from a Somertech kit. This kit, containing small section wood, corner pieces and glue can give excellent results.

The activity fits in with topics on 'Machines' and 'Medieval History.'

Key vocabulary

ballista, catapult, firings, force, medieval, target, tension

National Science Curriculum analysis

Attainment target	Statements of Attainment
1	3a, 3c, 3e, 3f 4a, 4b, 4c, 4f, 4g
6	4a, 4b
10	3a, 4a, 4b
13	3a, 3c, 4c

National Technology Curriculum analysis

Attainment target	Statements of Attainment
2	3a, 3b, 3d, 4a, 4d
3	3a, 3b, 3c, 3d, 4a, 4d
4	3a, 3b, 4a

Raise the drawbridge

A challenge:
Design and make a lifting bridge which covers a gap of 15 cm. Use the parts from a LEGO Technic 1 kit.

Challenge 20: Raise the drawbridge

Specific aims:

To develop skills in designing and making.
To develop skills in planning investigations.
To develop an appreciation of the use of gearing systems.

Equipment per group:

- LEGO Technic kit 1
- LEGO building bricks
- centimetre ruler

Notes

The important part of this structure is the winding mechanism which can be used to raise or lower the drawbridge. Most children cope well with this, and many like to embellish their structure by building a section of castle wall round the gateway using LEGO bricks.

During the trialing of this activity, a wide range of designs were seen, the parts of the LEGO kit being used in some unusual and ingenious ways. Children were impressed when told that their design was probably unique with no one having built a device quite like theirs before. This is an ideal opportunity to point out to children that there is not one correct answer to this problem, but rather that many designs can meet the criteria of the problem.

As in other open-ended constructional activities, the process of building, testing and improving takes time but is well worth the commitment.

The problem can be extended to involve the building of a portcullis, i.e. a gate which can be raised and lowered using a winding mechanism.

As with Challenge 19 *Medieval misery*, this exercise fits well into a topic on 'Machines' or 'Medieval History'.

Key vocabulary

drawbridge, gateway, gears, winding mechanism

National Science Curriculum analysis

Attainment target	Statements of Attainment
1	3a, 3e, 3h 4a, 4b, 4f, 4i, 4j
10	3a, 4a
13	3a, 3c, 4c

National Technology Curriculum analysis

Attainment target	Statements of Attainment
2	3a, 3b, 3d, 4a, 4d
3	3a, 3b, 3c, 3d, 4a, 4d
4	3a, 3b, 4a

What a breeze

A challenge:
Design and make a device for measuring wind speed.

The best device will work
in very light breezes
and in strong winds.

Challenge 21: What a breeze

Specific aims:

To develop skills in designing and making.
To develop skills in planning investigations.

Equipment per group:

- hair dryer or battery-powered toy fan
- Sellotape
- cotton thread
- retort stand and clamp (if available)
- centimetre ruler
- broom handle
- bamboo cane
- dressmaking pins
- drawing pins
- cocktail sticks
- Plasticine or Blu-Tack
- strips of material, 20 cm × 5 cm, e.g.
  tissue paper   tracing paper
  foil   card
  polythene   pulpboard
  writing paper
- paper hole puncher

Notes

The variety of solutions to this challenge is limited only by the materials provided. It is an excellent idea to ask children to discuss the challenge in groups and bring in useful materials from home.

The main design problem is to make a device which is both robust enough for high winds and yet sensitive enough for light breezes. For younger children it would be better to have only four types of material, e.g. tissue paper, polythene, writing paper and card.

One solution involves attaching the various strips of material to a broom handle which is placed across the space between two tables. It is essential to ensure that the material is attached rigidly to the broom handle either with drawing pins or tied with string.

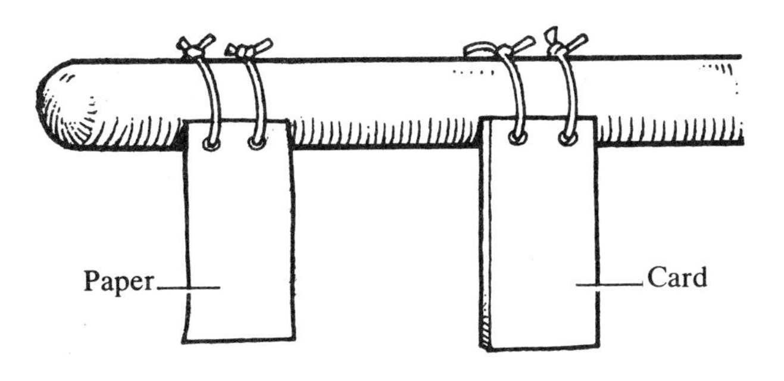

Using a hair dryer or a small fan children can then test which material is least resistant and which material is most resistant to the 'wind' produced. The degree of deflection of the chosen material can then be used to compare wind speeds.

The resulting machine can be tested outside in the playground on calm and windy days.

This activity has been used in topics on 'Flight' and 'Weather'.

Key vocabulary

breeze, hinge, pendulum, scale, sensitivity, wind speed

National Science Curriculum analysis

Attainment target	Statements of Attainment
1	1a, 1b 2a, 2b, 2c, 2d, 2e, 2f 3a, 3c, 3e, 3f, 3g, 3i 4a, 4b, 4c, 4d, 4f, 4i
6	2a, 3b, 4a
9	2b, 3b, 4a
10	2a, 3a

National Technology Curriculum analysis

Attainment target	Statements of Attainment
2	1a, 2a, 3b, 4a, 4d
3	1a, 2a, 2b, 2c, 3b, 3d
4	1a, 2a, 3b, 4a

The long drop

A challenge:
Design and make a parachute.

Your parachute must let a 5 gram mass fall as slowly as possible from a height of 2 metres.

Test your falling parachute.
(Time it at least 3 times.)

Then try and improve it.

Challenge 22: The long drop

Specific aims:

To develop skills in designing and making.
To develop skills in measuring.
To develop skills in fair testing.

Equipment per group:

- plain paper
- tissue paper
- plastic bags
- paper clips
- scissors
- Sellotape
- cotton thread
- string
- digital stop-watch
- 5 g Plasticine

Notes

This challenge has proven to be stimulating and enjoyable, especially where emphasis has been put on producing unusual designs. Children need to be encouraged to 'invent' a parachute made from different materials and having varied shapes of canopy.

After building and testing prototypes, children go on to modify and retest their new version. During this process, the idea of a 'fair test' can be developed and consolidated.

This challenge has been used in topics such as 'Flight', 'Space' and 'Air'.

Key vocabulary

accurate, air resistance, average, canopy, parachute, prototype

National Science Curriculum analysis

Attainment target	Statements of Attainment
1	2a, 2c, 2d, 2e, 2f 3a, 3c, 3d, 3e, 3f, 3g 4a, 4b, 4c, 4d, 4g, 4i, 4j
6	2a, 4a, 4b
9	3b
10	2a, 3a, 4c
13	4c

National Technology Curriculum analysis

Attainment target	Statements of Attainment
2	2a, 3a, 3b, 3c, 4a
3	2a, 2b, 2c, 3a, 3b, 3d
4	2a, 3b, 4a, 4b

The little twister

Make your little twister using this plan.

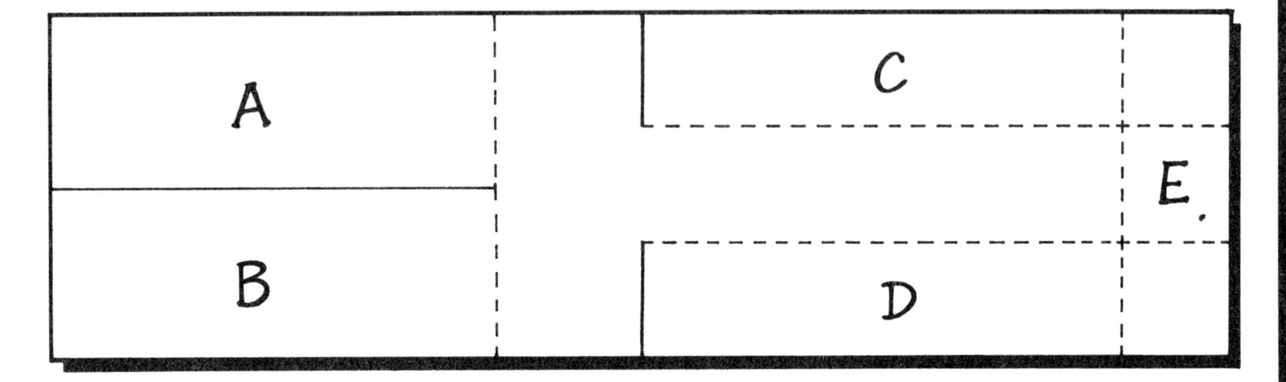

1 Cut along all the solid lines.

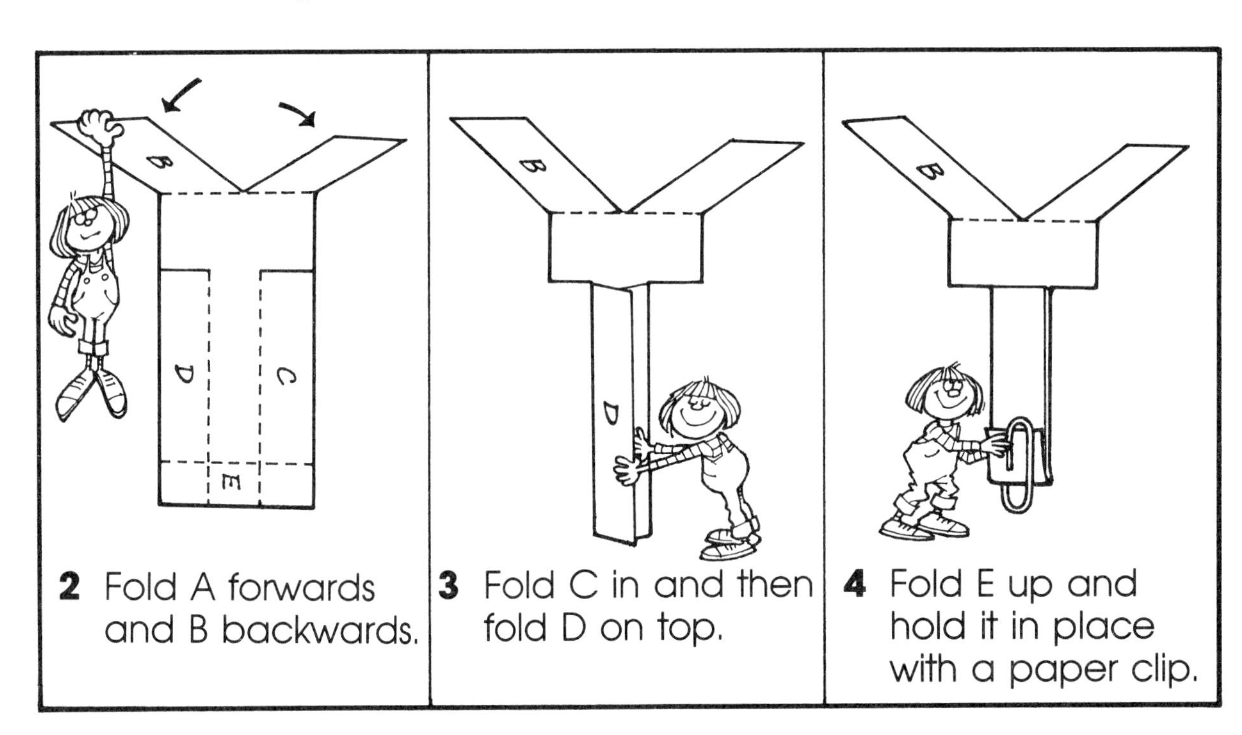

2 Fold A forwards and B backwards.

3 Fold C in and then fold D on top.

4 Fold E up and hold it in place with a paper clip.

Test your twister by dropping it from a height of 2 metres.

A challenge:
Change your design to make your twister fall very slowly.

Challenge 23: The little twister

Specific aims:

To develop skills in designing and making.
To develop skills in measuring.
To develop skills in planning investigations.
To develop skills in fair testing.

Equipment per group:

- photocopy of workcard plan
- card
- scissors
- Sellotape
- paper clips
- Plasticine or Blu-Tack
- plain paper
- cooking foil
- centimetre ruler
- digital stop-watch

Notes

This stimulating and enjoyable challenge has proved an ideal exercise for developing children's ideas on 'fair tests'. Younger children benefit from having the design pre-cut from the sheet but most children can quickly get to the stage of 'flying' their twisters.

There are two basic areas where the design can be changed:
1 material used
2 dimensions of the twister,
and children should be allowed to investigate either of these areas.

However, problems can arise when they change too much too soon and so make a systematic analysis impossible. They need to be encouraged to make **one** change, test it and evaluate what effect that change has had. From that point they can make further changes, testing at each stage. Again, the average of a number of trial runs is much more accurate than one single trial.

A simpler design of 'twister' used successfully with younger children is shown opposite:

The challenge can be extended to look at seed dispersal with sycamore wings.

The little twister has been used in topics such as 'Flight', 'Air' and 'Seeds'.

Key vocabulary

accurate, average, seed dispersal, twirl, twist

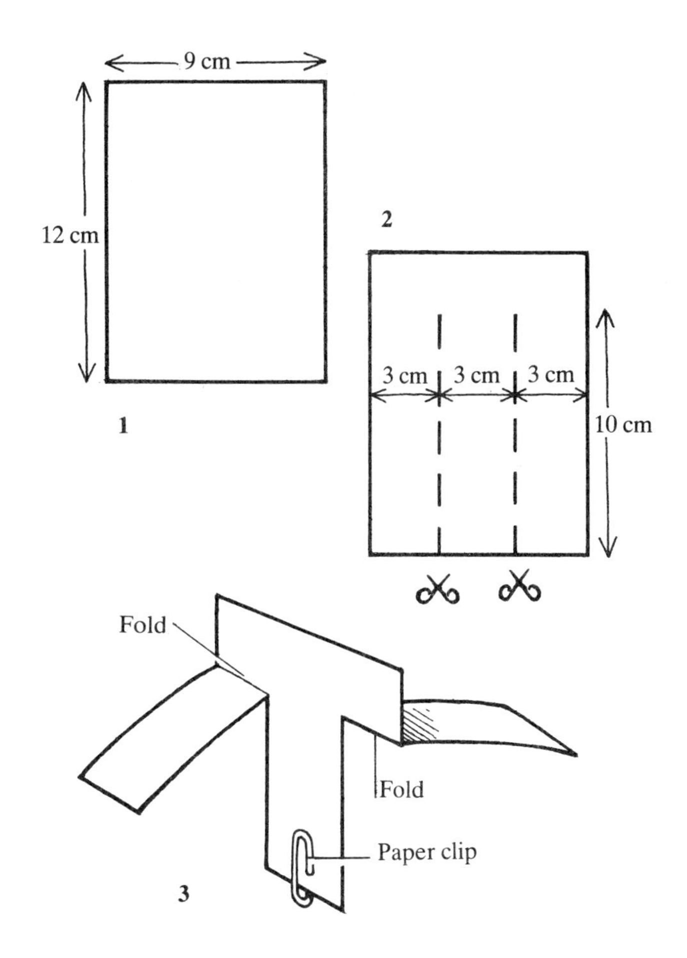

National Science Curriculum analysis

Attainment target	Statements of Attainment
1	3a, 3c, 3d, 3e, 3f, 3g 3h, 3i 4a, 4b, 4c, 4d, 4g, 4h 4i, 4j
6	4a, 4b
9	3b
10	4c
13	3a, 4c

National Technology Curriculum analysis

Attainment target	Statements of Attainment
2	3b, 3c, 4a
3	3a, 3b, 3d
4	3b, 4a, 4b

Flight of fancy

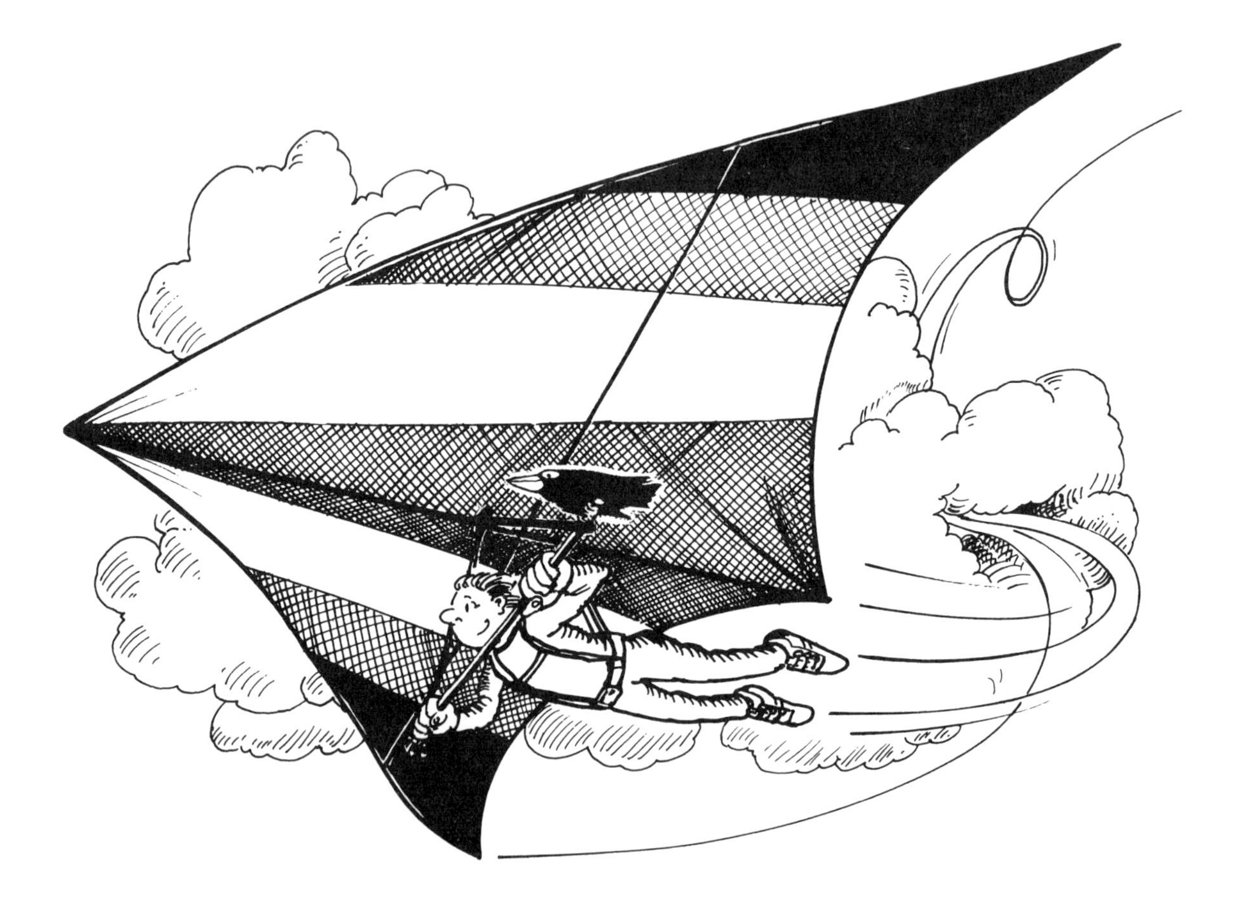

A challenge:
Design and make a paper aeroplane.

Your aeroplane must stay in the air for as **long** as possible when you throw it two metres from the ground.

Remember:
The fastest aeroplanes don't always fly for the longest time.

Challenge 24: Flight of fancy

Specific aims:

To develop skills in designing and making.
To develop skills in measuring.
To develop skills in planning investigations.
To develop skills in fair testing.

Equipment per group:

- plain A4 paper
- scissors
- Sellotape
- paper clips
- Plasticine or Blu-Tack
- drinking straws
- digital stop-watch

Notes

This is an enjoyable activity for children of all ages. The children should be encouraged to look at a range of different types of paper aeroplanes before designing their own. Unless children are encouraged to look at a wide range of possible designs, they tend to produce a very similar-looking paper dart. A number of types of paper aeroplanes are shown below and there are a large number of books available on 'making paper aeroplanes' which can be used to stimulate ideas.

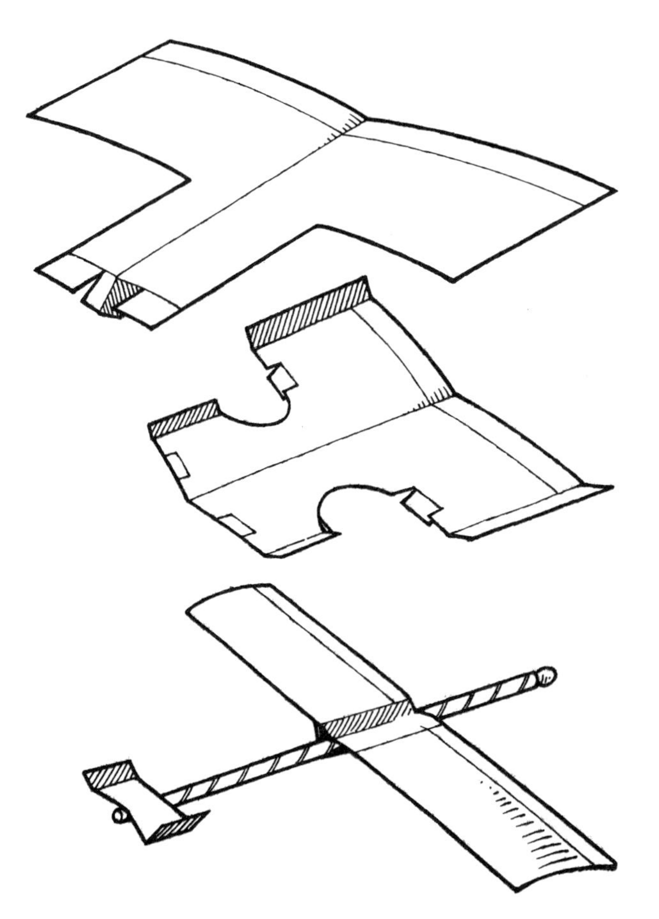

The children need reminding that the purpose of the exercise is to produce an aeroplane which will fly for the **longest** possible time.

Classrooms are generally too small for testing the models and a more satisfactory venue is the school hall. The hall stage is an ideal site from which children can launch their models. Again in the testing process, the idea of a fair test can be developed.

Once built and tested, the children can be encouraged to decorate their aeroplanes with bright and attractive designs.

Key vocabulary

accurate, aeroplane, average, crash, dart, glide, soar, stall

National Science Curriculum analysis

Attainment target	Statements of Attainment
1	2a, 2c, 2d, 2e, 2f 3a, 3c, 3d, 3e, 3f, 3g, 3i 4a, 4b, 4c, 4d, 4g, 4h, 4i
6	2a
9	3b
10	2a, 4c
13	3a, 4c

National Technology Curriculum analysis

Attainment target	Statements of Attainment
2	2a, 3a, 3c, 4a
3	2a, 2b, 2c, 3a, 3b
4	2a, 3b, 4a, 4b

The jet machine

When you blow up a balloon and let it go, it twists and turns through the air.

You can control the balloon by fixing it to a length of nylon line stretched tightly across the room.
When you let the balloon go, it can only move along the line.

A challenge:
Design and make a balloon-powered device which will travel 5 metres along a line as quickly as possible.

A good design will not damage the balloon.
You are only allowed 1 extra balloon if you burst the first!

Test your balloon-powered device.

Then try to improve it.

Challenge 25: The jet machine

Specific aims:

To develop skills in measuring.
To develop skills in designing and making.

Equipment per group:

- metre ruler or long tape measure
- thin nylon fishing line
- scissors
- drinking straws
- empty case of a ball-point pen
- Plasticine or Blu-Tack
- Sellotape
- cotton thread
- sausage-shaped balloons
- thin card or paper (A4 size)
- cooking foil
- digital stop-watch

Notes

The range of equipment provided is a factor which can limit the variety of designs produced by the children. A good strategy is to set the problem for children to discuss in groups, and to ask them to bring from home the materials they will need for their design. You will need to provide back-up materials for those children who do not bring anything into school.

One major design problem to be overcome is how to prevent the balloon being damaged during a run. Sticking Sellotape directly to the balloon weakens it. One solution is to make an open-ended box structure to hold the balloon during the run. The box structure can be attached to an empty pen case or drinking straw through which the nylon line runs.

Nylon fishing line should be used rather than cotton or string, as the nylon line is strong and smooth. The 5 metre run can be altered to suit the size of the room.

The exercise provides a good opportunity to develop the idea that a series of repeated timings are more accurate than a single reading.

The final part of the challenge asks children to improve their original design. One area they can develop is the streamlining of their shape, and provided they keep the weight low, the performance of most devices can be improved.

This challenge demonstrates the principle of a jet engine and can be used as part of topics on 'Flight', 'Air', 'Space' and 'Movement'.

Key vocabulary

accurate, average, control, device, force, friction, jet, streamlined, stretched

National Science Curriculum analysis

Attainment target	Statements of Attainment
1	3a, 3d, 3e, 3f, 3i 4a, 4f, 4i, 4j
10	3a, 4a
12	3a, 3b
13	3a, 3c, 4c

National Technology Curriculum analysis

Attainment target	Statements of Attainment
2	3b, 3e, 4a, 4b, 4d
3	3a, 3c, 3d, 4b
4	3b, 4a

A marble sorter

When marbles are made in a factory, the small marbles and the large marbles get mixed together.

A challenge:
Design and make a machine to separate the two sizes of marbles.

Test your machine.

Then try and improve it.

Challenge 26: A marble sorter

Specific aims:
To develop skills in designing and making.

Equipment per group:
- assorted sheets of card/cardboard
- assorted sheets of paper
- Sellotape
- scissors
- paper clips
- drinking straws
- assorted yoghurt pots
- shoe box or similar
- string
- selection of marbles (large and small)

Notes
The variety of designs produced by the children is dependent on the variety of materials available to them. As in other investigations, it is a good idea to set the problem and then to give time for children to bring from home the materials they need for their designs.

A typical design involves children cutting holes in the bottom of a shoe box, which are just big enough to let the small marbles through. The large marbles are too big to pass through, and collect in the shoe box. The smaller marbles can be collected in a container placed under the shoe box.

An alternative solution is to cut a large hole in the bottom of a shoe box and then Sellotape drinking straws across the hole to make a grating. The size of grating will control which marbles can pass through. The grating will need strengthening with Sellotape or string.

Steel gratings are used in gravel pits to grade the different sizes of gravel. In the commercial process agitation and flowing water are used to prevent the gratings becoming clogged.

Challenge 27 *Melanie the mixer* can be used as an extension of this exercise.

Key vocabulary
device, grade, grating, sieve, sort

National Science Curriculum analysis

Attainment target	Statements of Attainment
1	2a, 2b, 2d 3a, 3d 4a, 4b, 4i, 4j
6	2a, 4a

National Technology Curriculum analysis

Attainment target	Statements of Attainment
2	3b, 4a
3	2a, 3a, 3d, 4b
4	2a, 3b, 4a

Melanie the mixer

Young Melanie had a great time playing in the kitchen. She mixed together the lentils, dried peas, dried beans and rice from the kitchen jars.

Her older brother, Wayne, was supposed to be keeping an eye on her! Mum is due back from the shops in 30 minutes.

A challenge:
Design and make a device which will sort everything back into the right jars before Mum gets back.

Challenge 27: Melanie the mixer

Specific aims:
To develop skills in designing and making.

Equipment per group:
- assorted sheets of card/cardboard
- assorted sheets of paper
- Sellotape
- scissors
- paper clips
- drinking straws
- assorted yoghurt pots
- shoe box or similar
- string
- selection of beans and pulses

Notes
This problem is an extension of Challenge 26 *The marble sorter*, the main areas of difference being in the smaller size of objects to be sorted and in the larger range of sizes.

The principles are the same as in Challenge 26, but children need to look carefully at the size of hole they make. To get the best results, you need to select the beans so that each type is obviously different in size. A suitable mixture might contain rice, whole lentils, peas and butter beans. Gentle agitation or stirring is usually necessary to maintain the separation process.

This technique is used widely in the food industry, e.g. sorting eggs into the different sized grades, and separating the small, sweet peas from the larger, not so sweet peas!

Key vocabulary
device, grade, grating, lentils, pulses, sieve, sort

National Science Curriculum analysis

Attainment target	Statements of Attainment
1	3a, 3d, 3i 4a, 4b, 4d, 4i, 4j
6	2a, 4a

National Technology Curriculum analysis

Attainment target	Statements of Attainment
2	3b, 4a
3	3a, 3d, 4b
4	3b, 4a

A real smartie

A local shopkeeper needs your help. She is worried about a new delivery of Smarties. She thinks they are fakes.

She has given you some real Smarties and some of these new sweets.

A challenge:
Find out if the doubtful sweets are fakes.
Look for as many differences as you can.

Challenge 28: A real smartie

Specific aims:

To develop skills in observing.
To develop skills in planning investigations.

Equipment per group:

- genuine Smarties
- doubtful Smarties
- small yoghurt pot
- dropper
- felt pen
- digital weighing machine
- kitchen tissue

Notes

The aim of this investigation is for children to try as many tests as possible to compare the two sets of sweets. It is important that the sweets are not obviously different. Loose sweets similar to Smarties can be bought on market stalls, etc. but they tend to be obviously different. It might be better to provide genuine Smarties, labelled as doubtful ones, and allow children to come to the conclusion that the shopkeeper was wrong.

Tests which are usually applied are for taste, mass and colour. The latter can involve the children comparing the colouring dyes from the sweets using blots or chromatograms. Excellent results can be obtained, especially with the darker dyes.

The colouring dye can be washed off a Smartie by carefully putting a few drops of water onto the sweet. Children can then drip the colouring solution onto a kitchen towel and the colours will separate as the blot forms. Successive drops slowly spread the blot and the individual food dyes become obvious as different rings of colouring.

The activity can be extended to look at other areas where counterfeit products are marketed, e.g. jeans, watches, handbags, video tapes, records, etc.

It can also be used as part of a topic on 'Colour' and is especially appropriate when dealing with food colouring.

The technique of separating colours with blots can be used again in Challenge 29 *A fair cop*.

Key vocabulary

blot, chromatogram, colour, dye, fake, genuine

National Science Curriculum analysis

Attainment target	Statements of Attainment
1	2a, 2b, 2d, 2e 3a, 3d, 3i 4a, 4b, 4d, 4i, 4j
15	1b

National Technology Curriculum analysis

Attainment target	Statements of Attainment
3	2a, 3d, 4b
4	3b, 4a

A fair cop

A man was found murdered at the side of the road. Police are questioning 3 suspects but they have very few clues. The best clue is the note that was found stuck to the body. It was written with a black pen.

The police searched the 3 suspects and found a black pen on each of them.

A challenge:
Find out which pen wrote the note.

Challenge 29: A fair cop

Specific aims:
To develop skills in observing.
To develop skills in planning investigations.

Equipment per group:
- 3 water-soluble black felt tip pens
- scissors
- kitchen roll
- dropper
- small yoghurt pot

Notes
Most black inks (as used in felt tip pens) are made from a mixture of dyes, and it is rare for three manufacturers to use exactly the same mixture. However, careful pre-testing and the selection of a number of pens with obvious differences will allow the lesson to run smoothly.

One technique used by children is to make a bold spot on the kitchen towel and then to carefully drip a small amount of water onto the spot. As the blot spreads, the dyes in the spot are carried outwards. Successive drops of water will produce rings of colour. Children tend to add the water too quickly to the spot and the best results are obtained if each drop is allowed to spread before the next one is applied.

Ballpoint inks and permanent marker inks are not affected by water and will not form rings of colour in this way.

Another version of this problem involves investigating which coloured felt tip pens contain the most coloured dyes.

Children can also produce interesting artwork by drawing onto kitchen towels and then adding water to allow the colours to run and swirl.

Key vocabulary
blot, chromatogram, colour, dye, water-soluble

National Science Curriculum analysis

Attainment target	Statements of Attainment
1	3a, 3c, 3d, 3i 4a, 4b, 4c, 4d, 4i, 4j
15	1b

National Technology Curriculum analysis

Attainment target	Statements of Attainment
3	3d, 4b
4	3b, 4a

A box of delights

A challenge:
Fill your matchbox with as many different objects as you can.

Count your objects.

Sort them in as many different ways as you can.

Challenge 30: A box of delights

Specific aims:

To develop skills in observing.
To develop skills in sorting and classifying.

Equipment per group:

- a matchbox
- large selection of small items, e.g.

coin	hair
pin	bead
nail	match
paper clip	thread
eraser	nail
badge	rice
jewellery	lentils
ribbon	seeds
beans	elastic band

Notes

This popular activity is one which interests children of all ages. Children can either be asked to fill the matchbox at home with as many **different** items as possible, or at school if a wide enough range of items can be provided.

Once they have counted the number of objects, they can then sort them in as many different ways as possible. They could sort them by criteria of colour, shape and texture.

Children can often think of many imaginative criteria for sorting and this exercise can then be used to lead into further work on sorting and classifying.

Key vocabulary

classify, texture, sort

National Science Curriculum analysis

Attainment target	Statements of Attainment
1	2a, 2c, 2d, 2f 3e, 3f, 3g, 3i
6	2b, 3b
15	1b

National Technology Curriculum analysis

Attainment target	Statements of Attainment
3	2a, 3d
4	3b

Planetary puzzle

After months of space travel and adventures, Captain Kirk and his crew decided to take a holiday. They beamed down to a peaceful planet for a short break.

The planet is home to 4 groups of animals and 4 groups of plants.

Two challenges:

1 Make a key to help the explorers identify the 4 animal groups.
Choose a name for each group.

2 Make a key to help the explorers identify the 4 plant groups.
Choose a name for each group.

Challenge 31: Planetary puzzle

Specific aims:
To develop skills in observing.
To develop skills in sorting and classifying.

Notes
In this challenge, children need only a photocopy of the workcard illustrating the 'peaceful planet'.

The first step is usually to sort out the plants from the animals, and many children draw out the four different animals onto one sheet of paper and the four different plants onto another sheet of paper. To minimise confusion, it is a good idea to suggest that they concentrate either on the plants or the animals.

With the plants, children use characteristics such as leaf shape, flower shape, and presence of berries to separate the four plants.

With the animals, children use characteristics such as number of legs, number of ears and patterns on skin to separate the four animals.

Giving names to the plants and animals can generate a number of amusing and appropriate names.

This problem has proved very useful in consolidating work on sorting into sets and classifying, and it can also be used to stimulate ideas for children to design their own animals.

Key vocabulary
animal, characteristic, classify, identify, peaceful, planet, plant

National Science Curriculum analysis

Attainment target	Statements of Attainment
1	2b, 2d, 2e
2	3a, 3b, 4a
12	3a, 3b

The silver snatch

There is an exhibition of modern art at the art gallery.
One of the displays is a valuable silver brick.

A challenge:
Design and make an alarm to protect this valuable brick.

Challenge 32: The silver snatch

Specific aims:
To develop skills in designing and making.

Equipment per group:
- two 1.5 V batteries
- 3 V bulb and bulb holder
- 6 connecting wires with crocodile clips
- Sellotape
- sprung clothes peg
- 4 cm × 1 cm strips of copper foil or cooking foil
- drawing pins
- buzzer
- Plasticine or Blu-Tack
- scissors
- brick wrapped in kitchen foil
- small screwdriver

Safety note:
Emphasise the dangers of mains electricity and remind pupils that in this exercise they are using 'safe' batteries and bulbs as models. They must **not** go home and investigate the mains supply.

Notes
Children will need some basic understanding of how to connect up a simple electrical circuit with batteries, bulb and wire before they can proceed with this problem

The most popular solution involves using the clothes peg. The weight of the brick is used to keep the jaws of the peg open. Contacts made of foil are fitted to the jaws of the peg. When the brick is moved, the jaws close, the circuit is completed and the alarm is triggered.

A less elegant solution involves using the foil wrapped round the brick as a conductor. When the brick is moved, the circuit is broken and the bulb goes out. Unfortunately, the bulb going out does not have the same impact as the buzzer going on.

This challenge, and Challenge 33 *Take care*, are complementary and can be used together on topics such as 'Electricity' and 'Security'.

Key vocabulary
alarm, buzzer, circuit, conductor, connection, contact, exhibition, security, switch, triggered

National Science Curriculum analysis

Attainment target	Statements of Attainment
1	3a, 3f, 3i
	4b, 4f, 4i, 4j
6	4b
11	3a, 3b, 4a, 5a

National Technology Curriculum analysis

Attainment target	Statements of Attainment
1	3a, 3b
2	3b, 3e, 4a
3	3a, 3b, 4b
4	3b, 4a

Take care

Mrs Gottalot, a rich art collector, owns many expensive paintings. She decided to get the best security system for her home that money can buy.

A challenge:
Design and make a security system for her home.
Use a large cardboard box as a model of her house.

Test your security system.

Then try to improve it.

Challenge 33: Take care

Specific aims:
To develop skills in designing and making.

Equipment per group:
- cardboard box/shoe box
- two 1.5 V batteries
- two 3 V bulbs and bulbholders
- 10 connecting wires with crocodile clips
- Sellotape
- sprung clothes peg
- 4 cm × 1 cm strips of copper foil or cooking foil
- drawing pins
- buzzer
- Plasticine or Blu-Tack
- scissors
- assorted pieces of cardboard
- small screwdriver

Safety note:
Emphasise the dangers of mains electricity and remind children that in the exercise they are using 'safe' batteries and bulbs as models. They must **not** go home and investigate the mains supply.

Notes
This is an open-ended problem where the possibilities are only limited by the equipment available. It is a good idea to set the problem for children to discuss in groups, and so give them the opportunity to bring in materials from home.

The array of devices is wide and can include the following:

1. contact switches behind a door and a window (both can be represented by flaps cut in the box) which are arranged to complete a circuit as the door or window opens
2. pressure switches behind doors made by resting 2 pieces of foil lightly on top of each other. Contact is made when the pieces of foil are pushed together by the weight of a 'burglar'
3. window shutters, fences and gates made from cardboard pieces
4. lights to illuminate the front door.

The challenge can be used as part of a topic on 'Our home' where children look not so much at the security aspect of homes but rather the materials used and the design of houses.

Key vocabulary
alarm, buzzer, circuit, conductor, connection, contact, exhibition, security, switch, triggered

National Science Curriculum analysis

Attainment target	Statements of Attainment
1	3a, 3f, 3i 4b, 4f, 4i, 4j
6	4b
11	3a, 3b, 4a, 5a

National Technology Curriculum analysis

Attainment target	Statements of Attainment
1	3a, 3b
2	3b, 3e, 4a
3	3a, 3b, 4b
4	3b, 4a

The pull

Tommy Jones works at the steelworks. He sits by a conveyor belt all day, picking out lumps of scrap iron from the factory waste.

A challenge:
Design and make a machine to remove this scrap iron for Tommy.

Test your machine.

Then try and improve it.

Challenge 34: The pull

Specific aims:

To develop skills in designing and making.
To develop an appreciation of the concept of magnetism.

Equipment per group:

- strong magnet
- paper clips } mixed to form scrap
- drawing pins } mixed to form scrap
- gravel } mixed to form scrap
- assorted pieces of card/cardboard
- Sellotape
- scissors
- Plasticine or Blu-Tack
- yoghurt pots
- dustpan and brush

Notes

The best results are obtained with this challenge when a very strong magnet is used. Old loudspeakers are a good source of strong magnets.

The scrap iron on the conveyer belt can be simulated by mixing drawing pins and paper clips with gravel. Some confusion can arise with the drawing pins. They appear to be made of brass, but are in fact made of steel and plated with a thin layer of brass to prevent corrosion. Choose gravel which is about the same size as the drawing pins to prevent children making a grating which would sieve out the drawing pins.

A typical solution is to make a small archway with the magnet taped below the apex of the arch. The waste mixture is then spread onto a track of card and moved slowly through the archway. If the magnet is strong enough and positioned correctly, it will pick out the drawing pins and paper clips.

Another more elaborate solution is to fix the magnet to one side of a sloping piece of card. If the mixture is slowly trickled down the slope, most of the drawing pins and paper clips are drawn towards the magnet. Two containers can be positioned at the bottom of the slope: one on the magnetic side labelled 'scrap iron', the other away from the magnet labelled 'waste'.

The situation described in the problem occurs in refuse recycling plants where materials containing iron need to be removed from the rest of the household rubbish. This is done with powerful electromagnets, but the principle is exactly the same as that used by many of the children in their own solution.

Key vocabulary

conveyor belt, grating, magnet, magnetic, metal, non-magnetic, recycle, separate, sieve, steel, waste

National Science Curriculum analysis

Attainment target	Statements of Attainment
1	3a, 3f, 3i 4a, 4b, 4d, 4i
10	3a, 4c
11	2a

National Technology Curriculum analysis

Attainment target	Statements of Attainment
3	3a, 3d, 4b
4	3b, 4a

Lunchtime scramble

Dave and Sue have started a business delivering hot drinks and sandwiches to office workers at lunchtime. They use bicycles fitted with large baskets to get through the busy streets. It can take 20 minutes to get from their kitchen to the offices. It is important that the drinks are delivered hot.

A challenge:
Design and make a device to keep the drinks as hot as possible on the journey to the offices.

Test your design.

Then try to improve it.

Challenge 35: Lunchtime scramble

Specific aims:

To develop skills in designing and making.
To develop skills in measuring.
To develop an appreciation of the concept of insulation.

Equipment per group:

- assorted yoghurt pots/plastic drinking cups
- scissors
- Sellotape
- assorted pieces of

card	paper
cardboard	cloth
plastic	newspaper

- polystyrene ceiling tiles
- cotton wool
- digital stop-watch
- spirit thermometer
- electric kettle (used only under teacher supervision)

Safety note:

Remind children to be careful near hot water. Do not use boiling water.

Notes

This challenge presents many opportunities for developing children's scientific skills. Initially they design and make the container, and then they have to test how efficient it is. After testing they have the opportunity to modify their original design and then retest it. All this takes time, but it is time well spent.

A major constraint on this challenge is the variety of material available. If children are asked to discuss the problem in groups and then bring in some of the materials from home, the response is usually excellent.

A typical solution is to pack a plastic drinking cup into a cardboard box packed with an insulating material. Children use a wide variety of insulators from paper to polystyrene, all of which give good results. (It is the pockets of still air trapped between the layers of insulation which act as the most efficient insulators.) A tight-fitting lid is essential.

The efficiency of the container can be assessed by measuring how quickly hot water cools using the thermometer and the stop-watch.

The ideas developed in the investigation can be related to commercially available products such as 'Thermos' or drinks flasks, tea cosies, sleeping bags and polystyrene cups. It can also be incorporated into a topic on clothing and the type of clothes suitable for very cold countries.

Challenge 36 *A cool carrier* complements the work done in this exercise.

Key vocabulary

deliver, insulate, insulator, polystyrene, temperature, thermometer

National Science Curriculum analysis

Attainment target	Statements of Attainment
1	3a, 3c, 3d, 3e, 3f, 3g 4a, 4b, 4c, 4d, 4e, 4g, 4i
6	4b, 4d
13	3b, 4d, 4e

National Technology Curriculum analysis

Attainment target	Statements of Attainment
1	3b, 4d, 4e
2	3c, 3e, 4a
3	3a, 3b, 4b, 4d
4	3a, 3b, 4a

A cool carrier

Doctors in a hospital on the edge of the Sahara Desert need your help.

They have started doing kidney transplant operations. Most of the kidneys they use are sent from other hospitals by air. They must be packed in ice to keep them cool.

Unfortunately the road journey from the airport to the hospital takes several hours. The outside temperature can reach 28 °C.

A challenge:
Design and make a box to keep a kidney cold.

Test your box.

Then try to improve it.

Challenge 36: A cool carrier

Specific aims:

To develop skills in measuring.
To develop skills in designing and making.
To develop an appreciation of the concept of insulation.

Equipment per group:

- assorted yoghurt pots/plastic drinking cups
- scissors
- Sellotape
- assorted pieces of
  - card
  - paper
  - cardboard
  - cloth
  - plastic
  - newspaper
- polystyrene ceiling tiles
- cotton wool
- digital stop-watch
- spirit thermometer
- tray of ice cubes

Notes

This problem, which shares its aims and equipment with Challenge 35 *Lunchtime scramble*, looks at heat insulation from the point of view of keeping heat out of a container. It presents opportunities for children to design, make, test, modify and test again.

Problems with the provision of materials can be minimised by asking children to design their container and then bring materials in from home.

A typical solution is to use a drinking cup as the kidney container. A known volume of tap water can represent the kidney in the container. The kidney container can then be fitted into a larger yoghurt pot with ice packed between the two. The pots can then be packed into a box and held in place with a variety of insulating materials.

The children can measure and record changes in the temperature of the water in the kidney container over a period of time. The results can be consistent, especially if an efficient lid is made, with the recording thermometer fitted through it.

Initially the temperature of the water in the kidney container falls to 0° Celsius and then slowly rises to room temperature. The rate at which the water warms to room temperature is a measure of the efficiency of the device. This can be a long-running investigation which needs to be set up at the beginning of the school day.

As in Challenge 35 *Lunchtime scramble*, the problem can lead into discussion on commercially available products, such as cool boxes, freezers and refrigerators.

Key vocabulary

deliver, insulate, insulator, polystyrene, temperature, thermometer, transplant

National Science Curriculum analysis

Attainment target	Statements of Attainment
1	3a, 3c, 3d, 3e, 3f, 3g 4a, 4b, 4c, 4d, 4e, 4g, 4i
6	4b, 4d
13	3b, 4d, 4e

National Technology Curriculum analysis

Attainment target	Statements of Attainment
1	3b, 4d, 4e
2	3c, 3e, 4a
3	3a, 3b, 4b, 4d
4	3a, 3b, 4a

Radiator research

There is a bit of a problem at the racing car factory. The designer of the new racing car wants to paint the engine and radiator silver. The engineer wants to paint them black.

A challenge:
Design a fair test to prove which colour keeps the engine cooler.

Challenge 37: Radiator research

Specific aims:

To develop skills in measuring.
To develop skills in planning investigations.
To develop skills in fair testing.
To develop an appreciation of the concept of heat radiation.

Equipment per group:

- spirit thermometer
- 2 identical large tin cans with lids
- silver paint and brush
- matt black paint and brush
- digital stop-watch
- measuring cylinder
- newspaper
- electric kettle (used only under teacher supervision)

Safety note:

Remind children to be careful near hot water. Do not use boiling water.

Notes

In this investigation, children are working on two scientific ideas:
1 using models to test an idea
2 designing a fair test.

Presenting the equipment to the children makes the problem considerably easier. An alternative approach is to give them the problem and then after discussion, ask them what equipment they will need to test the paints. This latter approach can produce some interesting ideas.

A typical solution involves painting one tin and its lid silver and the other tin and its lid dull black. A small hole needs to be made in each lid to allow a thermometer to be fitted through. Then under close supervision the same quantity of hot water is put into each tin and the temperature fall in each tin recorded over a period of time.

Older children can extend the work by drawing graphs of their results.

The colour of a radiator is a significant factor in its efficiency, especially if it works at a high temperature. High performance engines and radiators are always painted matt black to increase the cooling effect. Household radiators would be more efficient if painted dull black; however, most people prefer a light colour scheme even if it means their radiators are slightly less efficient.

Key vocabulary

efficient, heat, matt black, radiation, radiator, temperature, thermometer

National Science Curriculum analysis

Attainment target	Statements of Attainment
1	4a, 4b, 4c, 4d, 4e, 4f, 4h
6	4b, 4d
13	3b, 4d

National Technology Curriculum analysis

Attainment target	Statements of Attainment
2	3a, 3b, 3e, 4a
3	3d, 4b
4	3a, 3b, 4a

Seedy solution

Mr Weedy, the market gardener, has bought 10 000 seeds of an expensive tropical plant. Unfortunately, there are no instructions with the seeds and he doesn't know which temperature is best for the seeds to start growing.

A challenge:
Find out which temperature is best for the seeds to start growing.

Challenge 38: Seedy solution

Specific aims:

To develop skills in measuring.
To develop skills in planning investigations.
To develop skills in fair testing.
To develop an appreciation of the concept of germination.

Equipment per group:

- 3 seed trays with soil/potting compost
- 30 seeds (wheat, barley, oats)
- spirit thermometer
- 3 black plastic bags to cover the seed trays

Notes

A typical approach is for children to prepare and plant the seed trays. They then cover each one with a plastic bag. Each tray can then be placed in one of three positions where the temperature is constant but different. Examples of suitable places are: in a refrigerator, in a cupboard near a radiator and in a cupboard away from a radiator. The ideal places are those which differ only in temperature, again to emphasise the idea of a fair test. The plastic bags are essential, firstly to keep the light conditions constant, and secondly, to prevent the soil drying out.

Once an optimum temperature has been found for germination, other factors such as soil type, moisture content and light levels can be investigated.

Once the seeds have germinated, they can be used to investigate such things as:

1 'Do plants always grow towards the light?'
2 'Do fertilisers such as "Baby Bio" really work?'
3 'How much water is best for plants?'

Key vocabulary

compost, fertilisers, germinate, germination, thermometer, temperature, tropical

National Science Curriculum analysis

Attainment target	Statements of Attainment
1	4a, 4b, 4c, 4d, 4e, 4i
2	3c, 4d
4	4a

National Technology Curriculum analysis

Attainment target	Statements of Attainment
1	3a, 4c
2	3a, 3b, 4a
3	3a, 3d, 4b

Over the top

Tony and Alison love going to moto-cross meetings with their parents. Sadly, the best viewing places are usually very crowded. Both children are not very tall, so they miss a lot of the action.

A challenge:
Help them to enjoy the thrills and spills of their favourite sport. Design and make a device so that they can see over the heads of the crowd.

Challenge 39: Over the top

Specific aims:

To develop skills in designing and making.
To appreciate how mirrors can be used to reflect light.

Equipment per group:

- metre ruler
- scissors
- Sellotape
- Plasticine or Blu-Tack
- 2 small plastic mirrors
- cardboard tubes (from cooking foil)
- washing-up liquid containers
- sheets of card

Notes

The most widely used solution is to make a simple periscope using the cardboard tubes or squeezy bottles. An example is shown in the diagram below:

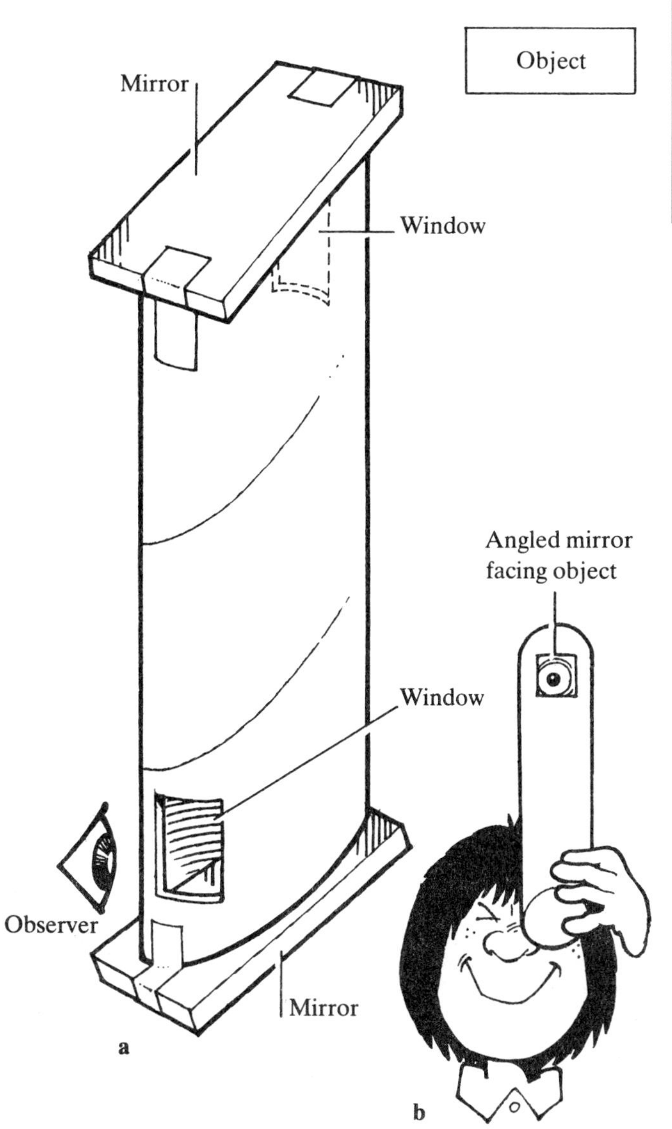

A solution requiring greater dexterity is to fold and cut card to form a tube to make the body of the periscope.

In both cases, care is needed to adjust the angles of the mirrors, although with a little patience, excellent results can be obtained.

Key vocabulary

image, periscope, reflect, reflection

National Science Curriculum analysis

Attainment target	Statements of Attainment
1	3a, 3f, 3h
15	3a, 3b, 4a, 4b

National Technology Curriculum analysis

Attainment target	Statements of Attainment
1	3a, 4c
2	3b, 4a, 4b
3	3b, 3d, 4b
4	3b

Eyesight examination

Different people have different eyesight.
Some people can't see near objects clearly.
Others can't see distant objects clearly.

A challenge:
Work out a way of testing people's long distance vision.

Take care to be fair.
Make the conditions exactly the same for everyone.

Challenge 40: Eyesight examination

Specific aims:
To develop skills in planning investigations.
To develop skills in fair testing.
To introduce ideas on short and long sightedness.

Equipment per group:
- metre ruler
- felt tip pen
- A3 sheet of card

Notes
One solution is to produce a card marked with different sized letters or numbers. The card can be set up across the playground or along a corridor and the children tested as in an ordinary eyesight test. One point to note is that the letters may need to be considerably bigger than on a normal eyesight chart to compensate for the increased viewing distance.

The children need to be reminded of the importance of fair testing, and ensuring the conditions are identical for every child.

The problem can be extended to investigate whether some letters of the alphabet are easier to recognise from a distance than others.

Challenge 42 *Standing out* is complementary to this investigation and can be used to find out which colours stand out well at a distance.

Key vocabulary
eyesight, long-sight, short-sight

National Science Curriculum analysis

Attainment target	Statements of Attainment
1	4a, 4b, 4c, 4d, 4h, 4i
15	4a, 4b

National Technology Curriculum analysis

Attainment target	Statements of Attainment
1	3a, 4e
2	3b, 4a
4	3b

Funny faces

Rose was given an interesting game for her birthday. It was a set of cards with faces drawn in different colours on them.

In daylight, the faces looked pleasant. However, when she looked at them through coloured filters, some of the colours looked darker and others disappeared. The effect was very funny.

A challenge:
Make a card with a hidden funny face.

Challenge 41: Funny faces

Specific aims:

To develop skills in observing.
To develop skills in designing and making.

Equipment per group:

- assorted coloured filters (approx. 5 cm × 5 cm) as used in stage lighting
- A4 white paper
- assorted coloured pencils or pens

Notes

Initially, children need to test the effect of viewing different coloured pencil or pen marks through filters. You might want to draw words or faces on white card with red and green pens and let the children view them through a red filter and through a green filter. Children can also test the effect for themselves using a range of coloured pencils.

Once they have established the effect of each filter on certain colours they can design their face. Through the appropriate filter, normally faint features will become darker and more noticeable. The effect can be dramatic when the eyes darken or the mouth changes shape.

An extension of this investigation involves writing a hidden message in a jumble of multicoloured shapes and letters. With an appropriate filter, one colour will stand out from the rest and the message will become visible. Some children may be able to devise a message which says one thing through a green filter and something entirely different through a red filter.

Key vocabulary

features, filter, message

National Science Curriculum analysis

Attainment target	Statements of Attainment
1	2a, 2b, 2d 3a, 3h
15	2a, 2b, 4a

National Technology Curriculum analysis

Attainment target	Statements of Attainment
2	2a, 3b, 4a
3	2a, 4b
4	2a, 3b

Standing out

Well done!

You have got the job of Publicity Officer for the next Youth Club disco.

A challenge:
Design and make an eye-catching poster for the disco.

Before you choose the colours for your design, find out which colours stand out best on different coloured backgrounds. Use the most eye-catching colours to make your poster.

Challenge 42: Standing out

Specific aims:

To develop skills in planning investigations.
To develop skills in fair testing.
To develop skills in observing.

Equipment per group:

- range of felt tip pens
- range of coloured paper/card
- metre ruler

Notes

Initially children should be encouraged to think about the possible colour combinations of paper and pen. With younger, less experienced children it has proved more successful to limit the paper to one or two colours.

The recording of the results is a vital part of this exercise and many pupils find a prepared table useful.

It is important to stress the idea of a 'fair test' and children need to be reminded that all conditions other than the colour combination need to be kept contant.

This activity can be extended by asking the children to find out which colour combinations are easier to see in the dark. They could construct a simple dark room using a shoe box.

The work leads naturally to topics dealing with safety (e.g. armbands and sashes for cyclists and motorcyclists).

Extension activities in this area can involve testing a group of commercially made safety clothing to see which is the most effective.

Further extension investigations can involve finding out about camouflage and designing clothes suitable for certain environments, e.g. desert, snowy wastes and jungle.

Key vocabulary

camouflage, combination, eye-catching

National Science Curriculum analysis

Attainment target	Statements of Attainment
1	4a, 4b, 4c, 4d, 4h, 4i
15	4a, 4b

National Technology Curriculum analysis

Attainment target	Statements of Attainment
1	3a, 4e
2	3b, 4a
4	3b

Pen colours

Background colours		Red	Orange	Yellow	----------	----------	----------
	Red						
	Orange						
	Yellow						

Distance in metres that the words can be read clearly

The battle of the bags

Two local supermarkets are deadly rivals.
Each shop tries to get more customers than the other. A big argument has started over carrier bags.
Mr Slick, manager of **Savalot Stores**, thinks his bags are stronger than **Betabuys**' bags.
Ms Smooth, manager of **Betabuys**, disagrees with him!

A challenge:
Find out who is right.

Make sure it is a fair test.

Then design and make a carrier bag of your own which is stronger than the ones you tested.

Challenge 43: The battle of the bags

Specific aims:

To develop skills in designing and making.
To develop skills in planning investigations.
To develop skills in fair testing.

Equipment per group:

- assorted carrier bags
- heavy masses (1 kg)
- broom handle
- Plasticine
- string
- assorted types of paper, e.g.
  sugar paper
  brown paper, etc.
- glue or Pritt stick
- Sellotape

Safety note:

Stress the dangers to toes of falling weights. You may want to protect the floor with a mat.

Notes

One solution to this problem is to test each bag to destruction by loading it with known masses. A typical method involves placing a broom handle through the handle of the carrier bag and supporting each end of the broom handle on the edge of a table. Most carrier bags can hold about 15 kg before breaking.

An extension of this problem is to find out which type of carrier bag handle is the most comfortable. One solution is to place strips of Plasticine along a horizontal broom handle resting across a gap between two tables. The broom handle is then placed through the bag handle so that it rests on the Plasticine. As the bag is loaded with masses, its handle cuts into the Plasticine. Bag handles can be compared by loading each of them with the same fixed mass. Generally, the more comfortable the handle, the shallower the cut in the Plasticine.

Before children are asked to design their own carrier bag, they need to look at a wide range of commercially produced carrier bags to note some of the design features. This initial piece of research is usually stimulating and produces a wider range of designs.

A safer activity for younger children is to find out which carrier bag holds the most shopping. For this activity the children need to be provided with a selection of boxes, cartons and plastic bottles.

Key vocabulary

destroy, handle

National Science Curriculum analysis

Attainment target	Statements of Attainment
1	2a, 2c, 2d, 2f
	3a, 3c, 3f, 3g, 3h
	4a, 4b, 4c, 4g, 4i
6	3b, 4a
10	3a, 4d

National Technology Curriculum analysis

Attainment target	Statements of Attainment
1	2a, 2b, 3a, 4e
2	2a, 3a, 3b, 3e, 4a
3	2a, 4b
4	2a, 3b

The crunch

A challenge:

Find out which crisps really are the crispiest.

Make sure it is a fair test.

Challenge 44: The crunch

Specific aims:

To develop skills in measuring.
To develop skills in planning investigations.
To develop skills in fair testing.

Equipment per group:

- assorted packets of crisps
- metre ruler
- slotted weights
- equipment as requested by children

Notes

This activity is excellent for introducing and/ or extending the idea of controlling variables, and fair testing.

The simplest solution is shown below:

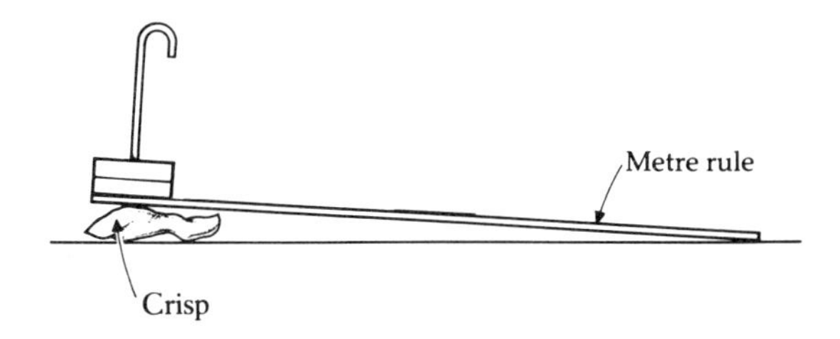

although children should not be constrained to this solution by the equipment available. If children are given the problem and asked to think about it and then bring any suitable materials from home, the variety of solutions is excellent.

One variable which is difficult to control is the size and shape of the crisp, although 'square-shaped' crisps which are now available from a number of manufacturers help a little.

An enjoyable spin-off activity is to look at which crisps are the best value for money. Be sure to obtain crisps which have the weight on the packet and remember the price!

Challenge 43 *The battle of the bags*, Challenge 28 *A real smartie* and this activity can be used in a topic on 'Food'.

Key vocabulary

crispiest, crispy

National Science Curriculum analysis

Attainment target	Statements of Attainment
1	2a, 2b, 2d, 2e, 2f 3a, 3c, 3d, 3e, 3f, 3h 4a, 4b, 4c, 4i
6	la, 2a, 4a
10	la, 3a, 4a

National Technology Curriculum analysis

Attainment target	Statements of Attainment
2	2a, 3b
3	2a, 2b, 3b, 4b
4	2a, 3b

A sticky situation

A challenge:
Sellotape is often used to stick materials together. Find out which material it sticks to best.

Make sure your test is fair.

Challenge 45: A sticky situation

Specific aims:

To develop skills in planning investigations.
To develop skills in fair testing.
To develop skills in manipulating.

Equipment per group:

- scissors
- Sellotape
- broom handle
- cotton thread
- hole punch
- digital stop-watch
- assorted types of paper, e.g.
  writing paper
  sugar paper
  card, etc.
- balsa wood
- fabrics
- cooking foil
- slotted weights and hanger

Notes

This is an activity which needs careful thought and preparation to ensure the test is fair. One solution involves using a fixed length of Sellotape and folding one end of it, as shown in figure **a**, around the hanger of the masses. This leaves a sticky surface exposed whose area can be kept constant from one test to the other. The exposed sticky area of Sellotape can then be stuck to the material to be tested (held vertically by one of the group) and masses added to the hanger until the Sellotape is pulled off.

Another solution, shown in figure **b**, involves draping the material to be tested over a broom handle and then joining the two ends with a strip of Sellotape (constant length). Masses can then be hung over the Sellotape until the joint breaks.

Key vocabulary

sticky, surface

National Science Curriculum analysis

Attainment target	Statements of Attainment
1	3a, 3c, 3e, 3f, 3g, 3h 4b, 4c, 4i
6	2a, 4a, 4b
10	3a

National Technology Curriculum analysis

Attainment target	Statements of Attainment
3	3a, 3d, 4b
4	3b

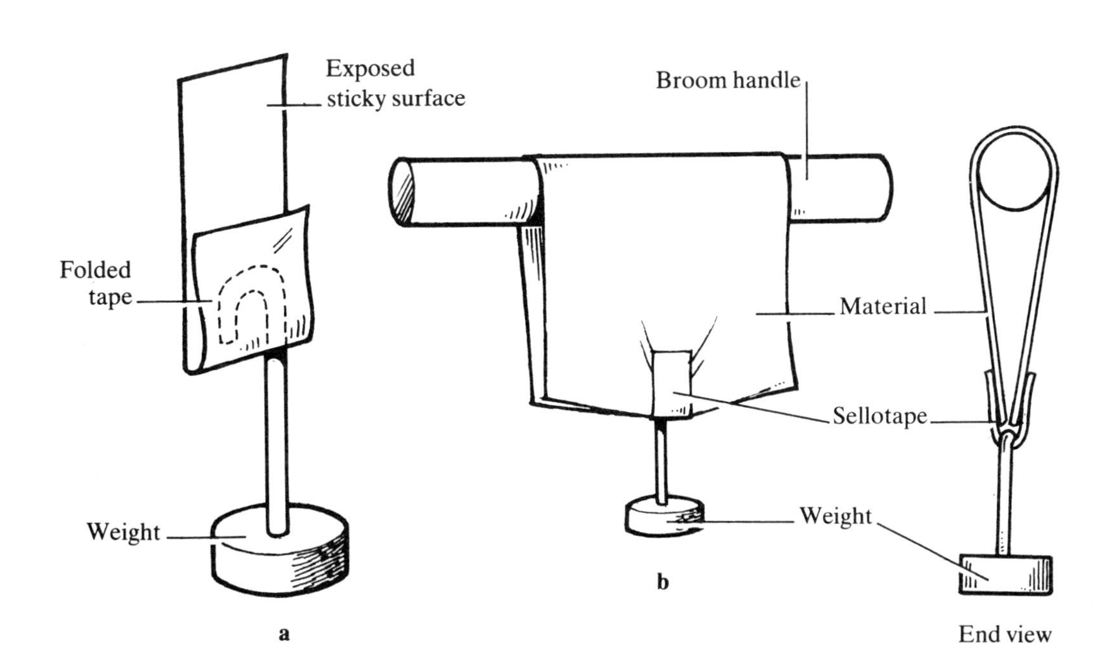

a

b

End view

A teddy bear's picnic

Teddy has been invited to a picnic.
It looks as if it might rain so he wants to take a hat.

A challenge:
Make Teddy a hat which:

1 fits him,
2 is smart,
3 and is waterproof.

Challenge 46: A teddy bear's picnic

Specific aims:

To develop skills in designing and making.
To develop skills in planning investigations.
To develop an awareness of the properties of various materials.

Equipment per group:

- a teddy!
- sheets of paper and card
- a variety of fabrics
- sheets of polythene
- stapler
- Sellotape
- scissors
- glue or Pritt stick
- water (for testing)
- dropper
- candle (to make paper and fabrics waterproof)

Notes

This extremely popular activity is suitable for all ages in the primary range. The criteria can be changed for younger children so that they only have to consider the first and second parts of the challenge.

Older children should be encouraged to test the range of materials for their water absorption properties before designing the hat. Also, originality of design as a criterion can be added to the challenge for older children.

An extension to this activity could be to make a hat for a giant. This will encourage the development of co-operative group work.

Key vocabulary

absorb, picnic, waterproof

National Science Curriculum analysis

Attainment target	Statements of Attainment
1	1a, 1b 2a, 2b, 2d 3a, 3c, 3d
6	2a, 3b, 4a, 4b
9	2b

National Technology Curriculum analysis

Attainment target	Statements of Attainment
1	1a, 1b, 2a, 2c, 3a, 4e
3	1a, 2a, 2b, 3d, 4b
4	1a, 2a, 3b, 4a

Scrambled egg

The Royal Society for the Protection of Birds has a problem. A female osprey has deserted her nest and left two eggs. The nearest incubator, to keep the eggs alive, is 50 miles away along a bumpy winding track.

A challenge:
Design and make a container to protect the eggs on their bumpy journey.
Find a way of testing your container, perhaps with hens' eggs, before the precious osprey eggs are put in it.

Challenge 47: Scrambled egg

Specific aims:
To develop skills in designing and making.

Equipment per group:
- paper
- card
- cotton wool
- assorted pieces of polystyrene
- newspaper
- examples of commercial packaging, e.g.
  bubble sheets
  straw
  polystyrene chips, etc.
- Sellotape
- scissors
- small cardboard box (shoebox)
- 1 hen's egg

Notes
This activity should not be restricted by the equipment presented to children. A useful approach is to set the problem, allow the children to discuss it and then bring in useful materials from home.

Many of the designs can be very effective, some surviving repeated testing. One effective test, used during trialling, was to drop the package from 2 metres onto soft grass. The severity of the testing can be increased by increasing the height of the drop.

Most designs involve packing the egg into the centre of the box, surrounded by different layers of material to absorb the shocks. It is essential to minimise the movement of the egg within the packaging. Modern packaging materials, such as polystyrene chips, are shown to be very effective.

A possible extension of this activity would be to devise packaging suitable to send a fragile parcel through the post.

Key vocabulary
incubator, osprey, packaging

National Science Curriculum analysis

Attainment target	Statements of Attainment
1	3a, 3c, 3h, 3i
	4a, 4b, 4c, 4d, 4i
6	3a, 4a, 4b
10	3a, 4b, 4c

National Technology Curriculum analysis

Attainment target	Statements of Attainment
2	3a, 3b, 3e, 4a, 4d
3	3b, 3d, 4b
4	3b, 4b

Bubble trouble

A challenge:

Find out which soapy liquid is the best for making bubbles.

Make sure your test is fair.

Challenge 48: Bubble trouble

Specific aims:

To develop skills in planning investigations.
To develop skills in fair testing.

Equipment per group:

- yoghurt pots
- dropper
- washing-up liquid
- shampoo
- soap
- soap powder
- bubble bath liquid
- plastic blowers (from bubble kits)
- thin wire (for children to make their own blowers)

Notes

This activity works well with children of all ages. With younger children it has proved useful to use only one kind of liquid and test the different concentrations of this liquid. However, older children enjoy testing the full range of liquids available.

Spin-off activities can involve:

- investigating the shape of bubbles
- can you make a square bubble?
- is it better to blow or to wave the bubble blower? etc.

This activity stimulates the imagination of children, and the range and quality of language and artwork which can be generated is phenomenal.

Key vocabulary

bubbles, concentration, liquid, shampoo

National Science Curriculum analysis

Attainment target	Statements of Attainment
1	1a, 1b 2a, 2b, 2d 3a, 3b, 3e, 3f

National Technology Curriculum analysis

Attainment target	Statements of Attainment
3	1a, 2a, 3d, 4b
4	1a, 3b